Genesis: Seeds of Being in the Early Years of a New Jersey Jewish-American

Two early critiques of this book:

"In Genesis, Marc Zimmerman, born in Newark and raised in Elizabeth, New Jersey, presents a collection of his childhood memories within a Jewish family, where father and mother work tirelessly in their restaurant. Within his loneliness at an early age, he faces several conflicts asking himself deep questions that lead him down paths that take him away from his Jewish world and opening the way to other minority groups, reaching the conclusion that the human race is only one with different experiences, creeds and stories. Readers will enjoy following the development of this boy who from his earliest years questions the world around him and himself." - **Samuel Soler**, Quebradillas, PR. First public reaction to Genesis by reader. 8/8/2020

"Zimmerman's Genesis takes us on an exciting journey into a man's unique struggles, as his protagonist, Mel, reminisces on the highs and lows of his existence, Born into a lower middle-class but upwardly mobile Jewish family living in Elizabeth, New Jersey on the eve of World War II, he is constantly at war with himself. His many conflictive decisions and actions somehow bring him to a fortuitous fork in the journey of life. Walk with him as he recalls his early struggles with his weight, his introduction to a Jewish community, and most interesting of all, his ideological struggle with his faith. ... There is ... a certain sadness in this book — a tragedy that underlies the author's narrative [giving it] the quality of a true-life story put to paper in striking detail. The author ... attempts aligning the principal character's timeline with significant turning points in ... history. Minority migrant families struggling to fuce into a new culture will quickly identify with this book. In sum, Zimmerman pens an impressive work of fiction. The storyline is absorbing and educational, and the flow of the author's language makes it easy to read and understand. There is also a touch of humor and romance to this book."   **-That Reviewer.** *OnlineBookClub.org review. 17 Nov 2021..*

Genesis:

Seeds of Being in the Early Years of a New Jersey Jewish-American'

Marc Zimmerman

Library of Congress Control Number (LCC): 2024910275

Listed in the Catalogue of the Library of Congress: 1. Fiction 2.
Autofiction 3. Jewish American fiction. 4. U.S. ethnic fiction.
5. coming of age 6. short story collection 7. Memoir

LACASA Chicago Books
2120 W. Concord Place
Chicago, IL 60647
mzimmerman1939@gmail.com
Tel. 281-513-9475.
Website: www.marczimmerman.net

"Whence did it come? What did it mean? How could I seize and apprehend it? ... And suddenly the memory revealed itself. The taste was that of the little piece of madeleine which my aunt… used to give me on Sunday mornings at Combray…" **Marcel Proust**, Extrapolation from *Swann's Way*, Vol. I of *In Search of Lost Time,* trans. J.M. Enright (1992).

"The duty of literature is to fight fiction. It's to find a way into the world as it is." **Karl Uve Knausgaard**, in a *New Yorker* interview about *My Struggle*.

Dedicated to my grandfather, my parents, sister, nieces and great-niece,

To my son, his wife, his daughter and sons.

And of course to my wife, Esther Soler and the entire Soler-Ramos family.

But above all, this book owes its life and is dedicated to all the relatives, friends and teachers who were part of my life in my formative years, whether they are mentioned by name, pseudonym or whatever in what follows or not:

my Uncle Benny, my uncle Al and all my uncles and aunts...

my cousins Howie, Lonnie, Larry, Steven;

my friends already gone: Robert Folkenflick, Martin Goldberger, Bill Mangel, Fred Meiselman, Alan Paskow;

others still with us: Carmine, Debbie, Ellen, Fred, Leonard, Melvin, Michael, Murray, Peter, Susan ... others

To Ernie and many others.

To my father, mother and brother-in-law Elmer, gone so many years ago

To my sister Elaine, and my cousin Carol Zimmermann gone in recent days.

All of us will be gone soon enough,

Thanks to the readers for riding along with my writing.

Contents

Author's Note

In the final years of my academic career as a professor of Comparative Literature and Latin American and Latino Cultural Studies, I felt the increasing urge to return to my first love of creative writing which I had left behind in the ruins of nervous breakdowns and troubled, ultimately broken marriages in the 1960s and 70s. I knew I wanted to tell stories; and an initial sampler I published of my best early work, *Stores of Winter* (LACASA 2006) told me that even as I'd grown older now, I perhaps still might have the passion and "juice" to do so. However, the fact is I didn't want to tell just any stories that might come to my mind, but ones that had to do with different moments and people that had been parts of my life. In effect, wavering between the desire to write fiction and do the typical old-age thing of writing my memoirs, I decided to develop a series of books that would depict different phases and aspects of my life from birth to as close to death as I could possibly accomplish before I could accomplish no more.

Four other memoir fiction books of mine, *The Short of it All*, *The Italian Daze*, *Martin and Marvin*, and *A Mexican Maze without Borders*, already include material drawn mainly from the subsequent and more recent years of my life—and I plan many other volumes of this kind. However, in sequence, *Genesis Two Ways West*, *No Light from Heaven*, *Black, Brown and White on the Border* and *Managua, Mon Amour (Nevermore)*, deal with the period from 1939 to 1981, and constitute and constitute what is the first completed of the three cycles that should tell the stories of my life and times in thematic or chronological order.

My friend John Beverley has suggested I change the title to *A Memory of Illusions*, and he certainly has a point. But whatever the real title should be, the question of whether I will be able to do all or much of Cycle II and deal well with the rest of my years, is one which only time will tell.

Three major projects haunt my modest effort: Marcel Proust's *Recherche du temps perdu*, Karl Uve Knausgaard's recent six-volume series with the overly explosive title, *Min Kamp*, and now the auto-biographical but also socio-historical series of books by Annie Ernaux.

Obviously, Proust's masterwork is centered on the upper classes of French society, and what we have most in common perhaps is a kind of Bergsonian psychology or philosophy of time and memory—as well as some few shared aspects of Jewish sensitivity and insights into the psychology of love. As for Knausgaard, his six volumes about a writer writing a six-volume book is a brilliant river of words with many wonderful passages and incidents, but without any will to aesthetic cloture along the way. This is not a criticism; it is simply to mark a difference. I have often felt the need for such cloture so that many chapters and incidents in my life read like short stories; and thus far, only *No Light from Heaven* and *Managua Mon Amour (Nevermore)* feel most fully like novels. Only discovering Ernaux after she won the Nobel, I have found her work increasingly pressuring me to make social connections between my experience and the wider world, and to try all the harder to consider feminist perspectives in relation to what I write; born only one year after me, she also reminds me that time is passing and that perhaps I should write *My Own Years*, taking me to their near-end, since it is quite probable that my years may be through with me before I am through with them. Of course, two Jewish American writers, born in the same hospital as I, Philip Roth before me and Paul Auster after, have all too poignantly dramatized for me, in *Exit Ghost* and *Baumgarten*, how short my remaining time may be and urge me to parallel Ernaux by writing a book highlighting moments from almost all my years, ones so different from hers, in case I simply can't complete Cycle III of books detailing my last 40-plus last years.

Of course, I cannot claim that my projected three-cycle series can in any way compare with the monumental efforts of these writers I evoke here, but they are what I have been about, they are what I am still intent on doing. So be it. Amen.

But why should anyone be interested in reading books about different stages of an individual life so marked by bad decisions, compulsive behavior and, yes, to be honest, frustrations and failures? As someone who supposedly became somewhat of a minor social theorist, for someone supposedly committed to collective visions and actions, why is it that I feel compelled to write endless pages on each twist and turn about my bourgeois individualist identity?

Why do I write memoir fiction and not memory or autobiography or testimonio? And what possible importance or interest can any perspective of mine have in relation to what's important in the lives of my possible or probable readers or in the world as a whole?

Many of my friends have been amazed by the number of things I've had to write about and the stories I've thus far had to tell. Somehow, I see myself as not having witnessed or done so much, of missing boat after boat. The reason I've had so much to write about is that I've lived failure after failure—I'm amazed at my terrible life choices and alienations which have led finally with much to write about. It goes back to Tolstoy's words on happy families (or marriages) being all alike, but unhappy ones being unhappy each in their own way. And my unhappy relationships and experiences have provided the bases for the many stories I've had to tell. So I've written many love stories, but that's because they're most based on a series of countless first dates that never went any further.

Still, to magnify my experience, it has ever so often became inevitable and yes desirable to diverge from what happened or what I dreamed to project other possibilities that only have come to me as I sit at my computer pounding out memories and, yes, changing them, enriching and varying them as I go—ever with the Aristotelean formula that history tells what happened, but poetry or in my case prose can tell us what should or at least might happen.

The half-lives I've almost lived, the roads I've begun to go down only to end up someplace else, things I've almost lived as well as the ones explored in a certain depth have given me a base of experiences that I have mined and reimagined to make my work go beyond me. Perhaps this is my version of the negative capability as figured by Keats speaking of Shakespeare attribued to the Bard— an ability to identify completely with his characters and thereby live lives other than his own, an ability also to break through any rigid scheme to find … whatever might be found.

Let me be clear. I have no gift of expression, no lyric gift, no capacity to describe a tree, a leaf, a teacup; I can recognize these qualities in others, but it is my great frustration that I lack them. However, what I may have is a kind of negative capability that involves some ability to project the lives and words of others, so I can sometimes catch fire from them. I believe I can get inside at least some characters and even represent figures who are more intelligent, imaginative and articulate than I. That is the magic one can find in our illusions or delusions of memory.

It is out of my bourgeois, ego-centered self that I am able at least at times to reach out to understand and evoke other people and perhaps a significant part of the world I've known. That I can do this at least sometimes perhaps speaks to the possibility that others not completely locked into their class formation and epistemologies can rise through and then above their original positionality to go beyond producing some postmodern selfie, to evoke or point to worlds beyond themselves, towards other more collective worlds they themselves may not experience but can contemplate, learn from and (why not?) enjoy.

At least this is my hope as I spin my own web even as the lights dim and my own personal end draws ever near.

Here, in this brief introduction to this book, Cycle II and the overall series, however, I feel I should make some comments that directly pertain to this particular volume which deals with my earliest years.

The first four stories are modified versions of ones drafted during my apprenticeship in writing fiction during the period from 1958 and 1964. The first story, "Summer Camp Days," is a rewrite of several prior efforts to represent my experiences in several years of going to Jewish American summer camps in New Jersey; it was never published, but a version drafted as a play in 1958 was acted out by campus drama students in my first playwriting class at the University of California—a class described in *Two Ways West*. The second story, "Valentine's Day," was drafted in 1959 and appeared over twenty years later as "Valentine's Day, 1947," in *Descant*, XXIV, 10, 2 (Spring, 1979): 127-138. The third story, "The Little Boy Who Flew Away," was originally drafted as a radio play accepted for presentation in 1963, but never actually produced, on Oregon Public Radio. "The Landlord," originally written in spring 1964, finally appeared in *The Great River Review* 2, 2 (1980): 189-202. These latter three stories also appeared in modified form in *Stores of Winter* (LACASA: 2006).

One aspect of the four early stories worth noting is that they were all written from inside the young boy's world and consciousness with only moments that point to matters (an indirect reference to Paul Robeson, a direct reference to Sid Gordon and other baseball players in my New York-area world) beyond the boy's immediate experience and understanding. Another matter affecting "The Little Boy" and "Valentine's Day" is their perhaps exaggerated reliance on dialogue, a matter not surprising in works by a young writer who was mainly focused on playwriting. I should also note that these stories also reflect an extreme fixity with regard to point of view—something that was very much the dogma among creative writers who feared "contaminating" their works during the Cold War. But whatever problems and limitations these four initial stories may be found to have as examples of the craft, it still strikes me deeply fitting for beginning this book and my overall life cycle series with them if for no other reason than because they are based on the earliest situations in my life that led to my first efforts of fictional representation—and of course the fictional representation of my life is precisely the subject and heart of this volume, Cycle II of which it is a part, and the entire series as a whole.

An added point I should make, especially with regard to "The Little Boy Who Flew Away," is that, like many Jewish families in New Jersey, mine had somehow submitted to the pressures of celebrating Christmas, without only some slight peripheral reference to Chanukah. So there are Christmas presents wrapped in Christmas paper, and I remember I also received one each year clearly marked for Chanukah—and yes, my ever-Kosher mother had her menorah and always lit the candles. My own contact with Christmas was especially strong, since my mother's sister Molly had done the unthinkable by marrying a gentle and affable German working-class man, my Uncle Frank, whose house I visited every Christmas to celebrate the Messiah's birth with them and my Christian-raised cousins while my parents were at work in their restaurant. So, I was a Jewish boy who clearly knew Christmas, and in fact I was one of the major singers at our high school's annual Christmas pageant, when under the guidance of Mr. Voight, it fell to me to sing "Oh Holy Night" and reach that fabulous high note that makes me still a legend, believe me not, in my home town of Elizabeth.

All this specified about Part I, I should note how very different in method and character are the other stories presented here in Parts II and III, all of which were drafted in the past few years after I decided to do a book of fictions depicting my earliest years. These other stories are more fully historical and ethnic, involving an attempt to cover some of the most significant experiences of my growing up, including some small but growing awareness of the social, economic and political forces shaping experience. The only one story beyond Part One to have been published before now, "The Italian-Americans," appeared as "Maxine Lamberto," in *Voices in Italian Americana* Vol. 27, No. 1 (2016: 84-91); and, again in variant form, it was republished in my book, *The Italian Daze* (2017). However, even that story was designed from the beginning to be included ultimately and most tellingly in this book as part of the larger life story being portrayed.

In sum, with this book, I have now completed all the other books which constitute Cycle II and represent the first half of my life. It is my hope to begin writing as much about the second half of my life in Cycle III as my time, health and energy will allow; I also hope to develop several more of the thematic volumes which are part of Cycle I. It is also my quixotic hope, of course, that increasing numbers (vast hordes to be sure) will eventually read my books and see how they reach out towards themes and concerns that will resonate into the future in the oh-too-human struggle against the forces of death.

Thanks to my dear friends John Beverley and Alessandro Carrera, who have always encouraged me even as I created a bourgeois I-centered narrative on my road to perdition. Puerto Rican friends, Ángel Quintero Rivera and Roberto Márquez, helped me to find perspectives beyond my older and more Eurocentric projections. For this volume special thanks go to a new friend, Puerto Rico's outstanding writer, Edgardo Rodríguez Juliá, who related Bobby Thomson's walk-off homerun to one Dominican Pepe Lucasa hit for the Cangrejeros of Santurce earlier in the same year that Thomson hit his. I am sorry that I could not satisfy Edgardo's wish that I replace the noisy, clattering Venetian blinds with drapes. But Edgardo is a novelist and can do what he wants; I am a memoir fictionist bound by certain rather rigid laws, and the blinds must stay, because they were there and, yes, they were essential to the magic involved in my evocation.

Special thanks go also to Robert Jaffe, my friend from my Berkeley years who found the plastic ketchup dispenser ad, and who as a lawyer who long refused to retire has offered to help me establish and protect my right to use the dispenser as central to the cover of this book. And why did I wish to use it? Because for me, the dispenser and so many other objects in my work (a sculpture, a smile, a locket, a wig) function like Proust's madeleine, bringing me memories which then go through a variety of transformations leading to the fusion of memoir and fiction which it is my fortune and curse to have as my underlying focus as a writer and my overall struggle against death. Proust is said to have attributed to Ruskin the idea that "art can recapture the lost and thus save it from destruction." I guess that's what drives me as a writer and keeps me cooking ever deeper into my eighties.

I wish, here and now, to acknowledge my now deceased editor, director Roberto Cabello-Argandoña, of Floricanto Press for seeing me through this cycle of books. Taking on the writings of an older author with unlikely chances of commercial success and always likely to create multiple editing problems in his old-man fussiness and failing eye is no enviable task. In addition, Roberto took on the work of a writer who only partially conformed to his prime mission of publishing Latino-centered writing in a way that is accessible to working-class Latino readers. I wish I could have thanked him more before his passing.

Finally, I would be remiss if I failed to note that this second edition goes to press as war continues in Gaza, with thousands of Palestinians dead and no clear solution in sight. Somehow, I could not help but notice how themes emerging in my early years are not only seeds of my personal being and becoming but of an ongoing and deepening conflict that has festered over the decades and has now come to a new dangerous juncture potentially affecting U.S. world and Middle East power alliances, U.S. political alignments and politics, Arabic and Israeli, Moslem and Jewish communities.

Post-Holocaust Jews, whether Zionist or not, are now seen as perpetrators of genocide; antisemitism as well as *Islamophobia* are spreading and deepening, and the Israeli campaign seems to guarantee hatreds that will endure for decades if not centuries, making any solution ever more difficult to devise and win adequate support.

I guess I see my story as one representative of a whole group of secularizing Jews (Isaac Deutscher called us "non-Jewish Jews")—including many Jewish Americans of my generation who left their religion behind and, rejecting their own tribal centrism, sought to do good, progressive things related to other groups who experienced prejudice, discrimination and injustice. Most of us did not identify as Zionists; many of us were pro-Chomsky anti-imperialist/ anti-colonialist intellectuals who thought themselves above the religious and ethnic imperatives affecting so many. We were clearly anti-occupiers, but yes, most of us, and clearly opposed to the rightward tilt affecting and infecting Israeli and U.S. Jewish politics. Of course, we were also against Hamas and Hezbollah, and all those seeking to obliterate the Jewish nation, which, whether justly founded or not, was now an established fact involving millions of human beings. So yes, we blithely favored a two-state solution with guarantees to both sides. But no, we did not join other Jewish progressives in Israel and the world who sought to fight against the growingly repressive, rightwing, and often racist drift of many Israelis and their unilateral supporters. We opposed but stood on the sidelines as settlements grew on the West Bank and as the Gaza occupation made life all but impossible for Palestinas, as Trump declared Jerusalem the capital of Israel, as the Abraham accords went forward without the slightest Palestinian input, and as Biden sought to extend the accords to Saudi Arabia. And now, we feel ourselves somehow complicit in not having joined the struggle against the Israeli right, in not having fought more forcefully for Palestinian as well as Israeli rights. And now the war continues, and our worst possible nightmares become reality.

Several of the problems adumbrated in *Genesis* have come to fruition; and unfortunately, the boy and young man portrayed here, even as he grew into adulthood, failed to find and to this day has not found adequate solutions to problems rooted deep in history and reaching new, terrible levels as I write these words. I suppose my book and my life stand as testimony to a seemingly promising but ultimately failed road in the time I've lived. May such thoughts as those expressed here help at least a bit in finding and finally building better roads as soon as possible. So I hope. Amen.

San Juan, Puerto Rico. 4/21/2020; revised 06/14/024.

Invocation

"Pull out his eyes, apologize…" Joyce, *Portrait of the Artist*.

1. And Then There was Light

Newark. A picket fence, dark green, small spaces in between. The staircase in a hallway, his mother and mean aunt washing the steps, his mother's hair more streaked with grey than his aunt's—further up the stairs, telling him something he can't quite grasp but which makes him afraid. Seeing cousin Dossie in her apartment by the window across the air shaft, eating spaghetti—him eating from the same spaghetti pot too, but with green peppers which kill his pleasure.

He remembers sirens going off, he sees Al Duglin with his air-raid warden hat and he hides under the bed after hearing that the gooseteppers have landed in New York and will soon break into their apartment to carry him off.

Outside the window, Dad has a new car, a Buick, with a fan on the dashboard. Al disappeared never to return, they said; his wife Minnie and their boys move to a poorer neighborhood… Soon, mother said, they'd be moving too… "Do we have to?"

Sitting in nusery school class, having to go, closing his eyes, saying it's a dream, the smell, students laughing, a man cleaning his body, saying *I thought you were a man*, sending him home from school in clothes that made his nasty aunt strip and spank him. *Disgusting*, she said, wiping him off. Another day, he was with Bobby Pearl, they break a bottle, a piece of glass gets in his eye, his mother comes to school, tells him, *leave my son alone.*

2. Pennington Street

They moved from Hunterdon Street in Newark to Pennington Street in Elizabeth—a move up someone said, as his dad took him in the

Buick over to the big new house with a huge yard behind—not too far from the store front catering kitchen he and his brother, Uncle Al, had by now made theirs. Carl, Black with black beret-like cap with brim, painted his metal bed frame tan, put Dutch boy and girl stickers on the now tan frame, told him he could get in the car and play driver, *but don't press this button*, he warned him pointing. He got behind the wheel, but couldn't not press it—and the car crashed into the side of the house.

The backyard so big, huge. He and his cousin Howie played in a little section they'd somehow dubbed Madison Square Garden. Howie boxed with him, bloodying his nose. He never wanted to play with Howie ever again.

After school each day, he went to see his parents working in the catering kitchen they rented, and they taught him to cut carrots for the cole slaw. Once, on his way to the kitchen, he saw the driver open his pie truck and take some pies into a store, leaving the truck back door open. He ran up to the door, jumped in, grasped an apple pie, went racing down the street, his hands grabbing up and depositing great gobs of the pie into his oh-so-avid mouth, throwing the pie tin and box in the garbage, going to the prep kitchen and hiding out.

3. Summer Camps

Every summer, for six weeks, he was wrenched out of his world into a camp with hundreds of other screaming children. Each year trying but failing to adjust, and then returning home to try to adjust again. Eight years of this, because his parents worked long hours; said they worked for him and accepted his thanks, ignored his guilt, his hatred and confusion. He joined them in the conspiracy of appearing "normal," "adjusted" hiding his misery and tension. On Sunday visiting days, they worked and couldn't be there when the others were with their parents; they came up on Wednesdays, but these off-time visits did little to save him. His overt normalcy strained him so that he was thrown back on his sense of inadequacy and anguish…. They tried to show their love by lavishing food on him. Their guilt became his, ingested with each bite. He grew obese and suffered the rejection and bullying that were to come his way.

4. The Grandfather

The wart one face of his grandfather's wife who they told him to call Grandma, how it always burned him when he had to kiss her. During the war, grandfather had a seder at their house, and he had a glass of raisin wine—or was it prune? Then one day his mom walked in on the old lady forcing her dad to wash the stairs, said it was clear the old witch beat him when she found he had no money, and now his daughter and sons declared the marriage over and moved him to a home where they visited him on weekends, taking him for car-rides on old country roads. The old man came to stay at their house some weekends, and his job on Saturdays was to help him put on his tallis and yarmulke and walk with him to shul, while on Sundays he helped with his tefillin and played casino with him always letting his grandfather win per mother's instructions, but trying not to let the old man know he was cheating in reverse as he sucked on one hard candy after another and then turned furious and threw the cards off the table when he caught his grandson letting him win… But the day came when he couldn't remember his grandson's name nor his daughter's, and another day came when the old man died, and he went to the funeral to say goodbye. Philip Yosepowhich born in 19th Century Romania died a senile old man at 84, and his grandson imagined he himself probably wouldn't make it to the year 2000, though he was still alive, kicking and writing his stories in 2020 at age 85….

5. The Sister

Up until nine he was not alone at home. His sister took care of him, but she had ten years on him. A victim herself, she hated … and loved him. She hugged him sometimes, held him close. But made fun of him, teased him for being fat. She locked him in the closet, teased and humiliated him in front of her boyfriends. She killed him a thousand times; she also consoled him and resurrected him. He remembers always having to achieve, always having to do more, wanting to be a composer, dying alone and unloved like Schubert, or deaf like Beethoven, unable to hear his music. How Elaine taught him to make notebooks on composers and musicians. She made one resounding gesture—was it love? an effort to get him out of her hair?

It is repeated in all the stories: in one summer, Sophie gives him pictures of horses of an old man and the sea; Elaine repeats the actual act, in World of Love by giving him the locket, but gives him the terrible, predictive story of the grotesque fat boy in The Little Boy; Hirsh tries to give him pictures, which he rejects, only to steal... She gave him the music notebooks filled with pictures and stories of composers and musicians. She urged him to listen to classical music and continue the notebooks. Perhaps the most important (the only?) love gift of his childhood, it created a world for him. He went to Dresden, Leipzig, Vienna. he played piano, flute. he was the lonely Schubert, the miserable, homely man, loving hopelessly, dies, his works buried, unfinished... to be discovered by his love... or not by her, never seen by her, but found a hundred, a thousand years later... Or no. Discovered one day, the composer begging in the streets of Paris, raced to the concert hall to acknowledge the grateful applause of those who had formerly, and with glaring insensitivity, rejected his magnificent opus.

He remembers Paul Robeson dressed as Othello. They said he wasn't an American. Was it true? She was the source of all knowledge; he probably sought her in one way or another all through his twenties...But gradually he came to reject the Jewess and seek the Italiana and the Latina—Catholic but maybe converso under it all. ... his life was to be this search and the attempt, also, to free his self from this image—to reject it, to reject all images. Quite ethinc of him, after all. The boy who goes out to meet the world carries with him the deep wound of doubt and unlove—the wound that makes him so insecure, so needful of reinforcement that he cannot stand the rejections (which he increasingly inspires—and learns to seek out, as negative affirmation) and is sent scurrying back to the house (the source of the wound) in search of love and consolation.

6. Friends and Nearby Family

Growing up in this town, this street, so near to and far from New York City. The winters cold… dirty, city snow, slush, radiators, furnaces in cellars. Soon they moved to Canton Street, near Warinanco Park and Lincoln school where Freddie, Michael, Marty, Sheldon, Marvin and Murray, Alan, Bobby, Lois, Doris, Susan, (always Susan until Ellen) and others lived, played and schooled. He remembers who played baseball and football with him just up the street on the fields of Warinanco Park till it got dark. Starting even as the March winds howled, and their hands froze, they played baseball through the summer heat and on into the fall, with others joining them until wind, rain and cold were too much.

He remembers the wall ball games where he and Bob Folkenflick played against the façade of the big apartment building across from his house—not knowing that Robert's father was a lawyer and how he was preparing (no one knew it) for a fine academic career; he remembers the stoop ball games on the smooth steps in front of his next-door neighbor Murray's house, knowing Murray's father was a top accountant and how he was preparing to be a doctor. Murray, who was always richer and better than him—Murray who got his first bike before him, and whose family got a tv long before his family did. Murray who stayed in the top classroom when he was demoted to the middle level, probably suffering withdrawal from his bullying. Murray, whose family did so well they moved to a better house they built "up the hill," Murray, the first object of his structure of envy that would all but destroy so much in his life.

Except for Freddie all of them were Jewish, and as he grew older, the holocaust was just too close for him to feel comfortable with Freddie. He liked him but suspected him, drifted from him as the years rolled by, only to learn in near old age, that Freddie felt rejected by Mel and his growing ties with what was at first an exclusively Jewish group, even as Freddie, always popular, always friendly, always competent and trustworthy, went on to be the class president, and as Mel commented at his high school class's fiftieth reunion, he was still class president and would be until the end of both their lives.

Near the park where he could walk or ride his bike across to Roselle Village to take care of his young cousins Bobby and Elinor and listen to classical music with his Aunt Belle. Later, he got to know the stranger who married his sister and then their children, Adrienne a little girl he babysat for, and Joanne, too young for him to take on that role, and then they moved to California and were gone.

Always to this day, he sees the house of the landlord, the short way to the park, the longer walk to the school park and the school. he sees the bushes, the front stoop. He sees the dark house, the hallways, his room. He hears classical music, the crash of the landlord (a broomstick against the rugless floor?) when the noise is too great. The bed _did_ break, he, his mother, different people, different times crashed into his room, terrifying him, filling him with rage, fear, hatred. And yet in the room, he always fantasized a girl's presence—a girl to share his tent (he made it stringing his blanket from the high bed posts—the site of his first wonderful masturbations). Through his window he could see into Murray's house, often see him with his family. He often shut the shade and then Murray, who was always number one, would cease to exist. He hung pinups on the wall and tried to fly away.

7. Early Loves

He loved Susan for years. She called him fatso, joined the children chasing him home from school. he did not stop loving her for many years. Always loving Susan who laughed at him when he tried to kiss her, and told him to go away because he was fat, but was nicer to him when he lost weight.

He copied and sent her a love letter Beethoven wrote and which he had read in his sister's notebook: "Last night, en route to Vienna, our coach stuck in the mud… the horses…"

He loved her and she hurt him so much, gave away a locket he gave her. She so beautiful, hating her, but not very pretty as a teen, flat-chested, skinny. He invited her out but then couldn't resist standing her up, avenging himself for all she had made him suffer as a boy.

Then came Ellen above all, and others like Maxine, and still the other girls of those early years. Failure followed failure, then came the Italians, the African Americans, the jazz and so much more as his teens moved toward their end.

8. Religion, Israel and the Bar Mitzvah

He remembers Hebrew School and Rabbi Golub, and how the children made fun of him year after year for being fat, for having a fat restaurant-owning dad. His father huge, terrible, always so calm till he took off his belt and filled him with terror… he feels the terror even now. He remembers the Sunday school stories Rabbi Golub told. And he remembers when he first learned how millions and millions had died in concentration camps, and how so many hated him and those he loved. Then he remembers his terrible letter about the Rosenbergs, which appeared in New York's hot-selling rag, enraging his family and shaming him for years to come. And he also remembers how they established the state of Israel—with him going door to door with their charity can to ask for donations to finance the planting of trees in the Negev, coming home to his now sisterless house to eat ketchup and apple sauce sandwiches when there was nothing else.

And in the midst of it all, he realized now that his wondrous story-telling rabbi (he of the deep Biblical-souding voice) was more of a sales than he was a wise man like those great ones of Talmudic days, and that, now doubting God Himself, he should by no means go through with the bogus bar mitzvah ceremony, but did so, looking fervent and spiritual in the photos he still has of it all …

9. Writing

It was his sister's notebooks that led him to try creating music or write more complex notebook entries on composers and musicians. By thirteen, he had half-drafted an opera script. But except for one haunting melody, the music failed to happen—because if there was a gift it was a small one not so much with words but the interactions and worlds they could evoke. Increasingly, he left aside his other classes to focus on those involving his writing.

And this in turn led his teachers to rank him below the brightest students who were roughly his peers, and send him from the advanced to the intermediate-level classes at the school.

He would never forget his sense of outrage and humiliation at being judged negatively, how he swore he would dig himself out of this hole and how he did it, day by day. And this would become his struggle, he sensed, throughout his life.

It was then that the interest in music slid over to writing which began to take over his waking hours—above all when he was struck with walking pneumonia, quarantined and forced to stay at home for three weeks. All alone all day every day, he wrote one prose-poem after another. Then he finally drafted his analysis of God and religion and realized that He didn't exist and that all his fervent religious training and his love of Bible stories told by his oh so histrionic rabbi were just a pretext for him to be a good young post-Holacaust New Jersey Jewish boy, surrounded by the others, and finding his way to high grades and the opportunity to go to college with the sharpest white kids.

Then, faced with a demanding project requirement to be fulfilled over spring break, he wrote a historical novel about the French Revolution supposedly with a fellow student David Kaufelt, who contributed three draftsman-like straight-line drawings and nothing more to the book—a matter which was quite aparent to this teacher.

Yes, he succeeded in recooping his status for the following year—and yes, he maintained his excessive productivity once he started at age 40, to publish his work. That is without doubt the source of his obsession with production, with his need to complete project after project, book after book until the final curtain would fall on his life—over-compensating out of his structure of envy, all to prove that he was not a failure, not an incompetant, at least maybe not nothing after all. An absurd fight always lost in the first round, leading him to produce still more, but to what final end? The same as everyone's.

10. Questions

Of course, it was David Kaufelt and not he who became a professional writer, while his own writing would go nowhere for decade after decade… And meanwhile the most intense love of his teens went on to her own career as a writer including work on themes that had drawn his interest early on.

Why the long hiatus between his realization that he wanted to write and the emergence of any published work, and also before his creative spark would finally light up deep into his allotted time? What dimensions of life and love, what problems and blockages in his early years and afterward kept him from developing as a writer all those years? And as a man able to face his life decisions with some wisdom?

But this is best explained by reading his almost completed (and yes eventually completed) old testament going up to the end of his 41st year, and then reading his new testament starting in his 42nd year and ending when he could write no more. All the seeds are in the stories of *Genesis,* which may help explain why he became who he became, but yes, they are his stories of before all that.

Book One. Boyhood

Summer Camp Days (1943-1951)

1.

By car, by train, by bus and then he was there—for the summers that would help shape his life and leave him lost for most of his times to come. How many years did he go; and each time, how soon came the moment when the powers-that-were realized he was not meant for this kind of life at all? He certainly didn't want to be there, but the walls at home cried out for more money and it was still wartime, so his mother had to up her work hours and that meant there was no one around to take care of him, and so, he had to go.

At night in bed came the great fear of the others down the row of beds. Where to pee, how to sleep, why their noisy sounds and movements, his own world so far away. Then the routine, making the bed, the hospital corners, the cleanup, the breakfast, the talks with boys from Boston to Philadelphia, strange Jewish kids from all over. Syrup versus serup, chocolate versus chauklet. Then the activities sheet, what one must and might do or be. Baseball, swimming, archery, singing… campfire, basketball, soccer, all the wondrous treats of life he despised.

It was always the same thing or something close to it, so that all the cases and examples of those eight years which, barring changes in his maturation and interests, could all be rolled or lumped together into one long summer.

There was Larry Lert, Ron Aronson; there was Warren Goldfein, a year his elder, with his long Jewish nose; Morry Cohen, with his huge club footed right leg, and a terribly skinny left-leg; and there was his med-student counselor, Herbie and Herbie's girlfriend, and there was Susan —one Susan and then another, and then Shiela—until one day it would become almost all about Ellen…

So many things to do each day, day in/day out, and he wanted none of it. He sat around his bunk, hardly relating with the other boys, dragging his feet during the scheduled, compulsory activities, refusing to play ballgames in his free time.

Until they began to talk about him, mock him for acting as if he were better, for keeping apart from the other boys. Until Herbie talked to his girlfriend about him—about how he was withdrawn and bitter and lost. Until she met with him.

"I heard you like to write," she said. "Well, I have these pictures I thought you might like to see, and maybe write up stories about them."

She spread them out along a picnic table. "They're woodcuts in black and white, so they leave much to the imagination."

Two most struck his eye—one of of a brave horse in full gallop, and the other an image of an old sea captain at the helm, with a determined gleem in his eye, steering his ship through a storm.

He was struck by the power of these images but he saw them as a kind of dare or perhaps an assault or insult, as if already indicating his inability to match the pictures in words, as if promising great shame should he fail the experiment which he would most surely fail.

The horse fascinated him with its fiery power and staring, accusing eye, but he could find no story of boy loves horse or horse flies off; and try as he might, no story came forth. Only the old man, his face a map of wrinkles from storm after storm, could speak out of terrible confrontations between man and sea, and all the whales and sharks, pirates and smugglers that had come his way. So he came to scribble out notes for story upon story, yarn after yarn. But try as he might he could not write the stories (as perhaps to this day he cannot write this one).

He could not get beyond a sentence or two scratched on the pad Herbie lent him to work on his stories; and the more he failed, the more he resented Herbie and Herbie's girl and then the more he suffered from his sense of shame and failure. And the more he sought his solitude amidst the ferocious socializing of the summer camp. And the harder he fought, the more aggressive became those who sought to woo him out of himself and make him into just another version of the other boys in the bunk. Before a week was out, he buried the pictures and notes at the bottom of his bunk locker, under his dirty gym shoes and all he'd piled over them.

The next week he found a turtle and kept it in a box he was afraid to throw away—a small razorback turtle, which became his friend and companion all his free hours, running along his blanket, snapping at flies and subject to his master's ways and whims. He gave the turtle a name, Merlin, found food for him, killed flies for him, told stories to and about him, found a bowl out of which he could not climb out, protecting Merlin from the frays of his bunkmates and the very eyes of Herbie.

The boys tried to join him in playing with the turtle. But he refused them, saying Merlin was his, all he had, the only thing he owned. And then one day he returned to the bunk to find it lifeless and already smelling however slightly. And he hated them all, suspecting that at least one of them had killed his turtle. And he buried the turtle and part of his childhood with it.

Just a few nights later, a new boy named Peter came to camp and told of the other kind of camp he had escaped from, of how his parents had died, how horrible the Nazis were. He listened in awe as the boy told about the cruel Germans, the Nazis, those who hated Jewish boys like himself. But he was somehow angry too, indignant that this boy was stealing his thunder, as if his pain were greater than anyone's as if there could be no doubt about that. And Mel found himself asking, "What about me? What about my terrible life and me? What about Merlin?"

Nothing could equal the pain Peter had felt. What had happened to him was so awful that it had somehow denied and robbed Mel of his special place. He found his throat and chest tightening, his temperature rose and pains shot through his legs. They sent him to the infirmary, and he wound up in a bed next to Michael, and the two boys talked deep into the night.

"I'm scared," Michael said. "We're sick and my dad—he's forty-eight, he could get sick and die, soon!" he said, and he started to cry.

Hearing his friend, he sensed what it meant to get old—to see parents get old, his mother get old, and yes, he himself get old. He felt Michael's fear and tears; he felt terrified lying in bed, trying tocce sleep but taking half the night to succeed.

It was the very next day that he ran away, resenting Peter, resenting Michael, hating everyone, mourning for Merlin. He broke into the thicket and ran along a path and then beyond the path, until, hearing the sound of cars in the distance, and fearing the coming on of night in the woods he raced toward the sounds, finally making his way on to the highway where cars streamed by and where, just as he was growing hungry and cold, the head official of the camp and his assistant picked him up and brought him back to the camp, each asking questions and he remaining totally silent.

2.

A few nights later in his bunk bed, he heard his counselors begin to speak about all the boys one by one, their goods and bads, their coming to him at the very end of the litany about the others, and then rehearsing his flight and conjecturing why and coming to the conclusion that he just didn't want to be with the boys, that he thought he was better—a writer though he didn't write, who kept the pictures he was given below his shoes that had now dirtied the pictures and that his notebooks showed halfhearted and failed efforts to write. He acted as if he'd suffered more than Morrie with his club foot, or Peter, with his parents dead in the death camps. What would they do about him? Should they tell his parents? They would be so ashamed, sacrificing for him day and night and him paying back this way. What would become of him, as he headed toward a life marked by the failures of these years? What would happen to this lost soul?

He felt outraged by their pillaging of his things, their dissecting his life. He broke into tears, and he forgot his turtle and mourned for the life that life had forced him somehow to live, and he moaned for his parents who'd sent him here against his will, but he loved them and wouldn't want to hurt them, and imagined the pain his counselors had conjured up, and now he swore that he would change, that he would indeed play ball with the others, and the counselors would see his great improvement, his great victory in the face of all.

And sure to his oath, the next day he began to change. On the basketball court the ball went out, bouncing down a slope, and he took it on himself to retrieve it. Out of bounds again, and he fetched and fed the ball to the players. Soon they were short a man and asked him as their only sideline fan to step in. Not much of a player, he was good at feeding the ball to the other players and even scored a bankshot of his own. His team won and he shared in the celebration. That afternoon he played baseball and caught a few and chased down the ones that went by him.

In the evening, they had a sing-out by campfire, and he lent his good voice to the singing until his counselor heard him and asked him to try out for the annual camp play. And sure enough he won the part as one of the Frank Butler's to play in the year's musical, *Annie Get Your Gun*, and practiced day after day to sing "They Say It's Wonderful," with Sheila, a beautiful redhaired girl who he fell in love with (she was his leading lady after all) as soon as they sang the song together. Rehearsal days came and went, he the perfect sport on the field, and the perfect team player with his performing group. At a campfire meeting they called a pow-wow, he was rewarded chevrons for good sportsmanship and teamwork and joined the campus honor society as a "brave"—only one more chevron and he'd rise in rank to scout and with still another to chief. Sheila did not respond to his attentions, but another girl seemed to like him as he sang the duet and she came over to listen not to Sheila but to him. When performance day drew near, his mother called him to say that she was coming to see the show.

Then came the day. And there they were—his mother and his sister too proudly watching until he saw them signal that something was amiss. He understood in a flash that there was a problem with the cowboy hat on his head, and he soon realized even as he sang that the string that held the hat was not where it should be on his chin but somehow caught on the hat's rim. Trying to act nonchalantly as he reached the climax of his song ("to tell you that love is grand, and with the moon up above…"), he raised his hand to his hat and flicked the string down, only to have it land square not on his chin but his nose, bringing the audience to laughter and Shiela to hiss and snicker as he brought his great declaration of love to its climactic end.

He was shattered by the laughter, looked out at that crowd, and he knew he was not like them, not even like his mother and sister, who always urged him to do well and to be governed by the rules of the game. And now he hated them and the rules, hated the counselors who'd lured him on, by his true loves who came to see him rehearse and who ogle-eyed him when he sang.

Some days later, when he won another chevron, he went to the podium to say thanks but no thanks, because he was unworthy of their respect and besides he no longer believed in their stupid system of honors and their phony Indian stuff and what did respect from the likes of them mean anyway? The boys hooted and jeered him, making supposed Indian sounds to drown him out. It was at this point that he stood up.

"Mel," he called out to one and all. "My name is Mel, and it rhymes with Hell and smell," he told them and then left the area feeling defiant and triumphant. He didn't attend the last awards ceremony but retreated back to his bunk and ceased participating in the games no matter how much the counselors and friends urged him on.

3.

On the next to last day of the camp season, Herbie's girlfriend showed up at the bunk to retrieve the pictures. They looked shabby and dusty, and she couldn't help but protest.

"But you've gotten them dirty sitting here in your closet. Did you at least try to write some stories?"

"No," he said defiantly, "I couldn't think of anything to write. I'm not a writer."

"I guess they were just too much pressure on him," Herbie said.

"No," the boy interrupted him. "I just didn't want to do them, just like I didn't want to play ball, no matter how you tried to fool me."

"Sorry," said Herbie. And he knew then he loved Herbie just as he hated him forever more.

The next morning, his parents came to take him home, and he vowed never to go to another summer camp. And he never did.

The Little Boy Who Flew Away

1.

Long before Christmas, Mel had stopped believing in Santa Claus. So long before that special day, alone in the house, he set out to find his presents, opening doors, closets, and cupboards, opening boxes and bags wherever he found them. At last, under father's bed, he discovered a cluster of packages wrapped in green and held with red ribbon and scotch tape. Carefully he undid the tape and drew out the gifts inside. Then, after seeing all there was to see, he slid the gifts back in as neatly as he could, retaped the wrapping and returned the boxes to their place thinking no one would ever know.

So, he was not surprised by the presents he found awaiting him on Christmas morning: the toys and games, the shirts and pants, the socks, and ties. Only one gift did surprise him, one he had not seen or foreseen. He had given out the presents his parents had given him to give them and they had left to prepare for the people who would come to their restaurant for Christmas dinner, and it was only then that his sister handed him a small package.

"Here," she said, "I thought you should have one gift you didn't know about." He took the present but kept his eyes on her face.

"I know what you did," she said. "You think I don't know about you just because they're not here and they don't, but I do. I know all about you. ... Well, don't just stare at me. Open it. You got so many presents—you might as well get one more. ... Don't tear it open. Take it easy for once. I can save the paper. Look how grabby you are. Look how you tear things up."

It was a book: *The Little Boy Who Flew Away*.

"Read what I wrote inside," said Elaine. He opened the book and read the words written out in large red letters:

"To Mel, from his big sister, who knows he will understand."

On the title page was a picture of a young boy so fat that even squeezing and squeezing, he could not wedge his body through a wide doorway.

"Thank you," he said under his breath.

"It's the story of a boy who liked eating more than anything," she said. "He ate and ate and got fatter and fatter. His parents told him not to eat, but he wouldn't stop. And one day he was so fat, he looked like a big balloon. ... See? Like in the picture. ... You can hardly see his arms and legs, or his head any more ... And ..." She flipped the pages to the back of the book where the fat boy was rising off the ground, while the others, the thin children, tried to hold him down.

"'And a strong wind came along and blew him up and away! Everyone tried to stop him, but they couldn't. The wind kept blowing and blowing, lifting him up. ...'"

She turned the page and showed him where the children and then the old people of the town looked up, straining their limbs, climbing ladders and trees. But no one could reach him. The little fat boy had become just a speck in the sky.

"'Look at him go. See him go,' said the people. "My goodness ... he's gone.' He flew away and never came back," she read to him.

"I'm not that fat," said Mel.

"You will be if you don't stop eating," she said. "You eat too much. If I don't stop you, who will?"

"I've tried to diet all this month. I've skipped breakfast. I don't eat all the food you pack for lunch."

"And what happens at dinner?"

"I "

"I leave you dinner and when I come home, there's no cake or fruit or ice cream in the whole house. Sometimes there's no bread left. ... I can't even make a sandwich for you to take to school."

"It isn't my fault you go out so much. You should stay home with me more. Mother says so. Then I wouldn't eat so much. You could stop me then."

"I can't stay with you all the time. I have meetings at school. I like to go to dances." He hung his head. "Oh, I know you don't like eating alone. There's no one forcing you not to either. You just eat to pass the time. First you take a little piece of pie, so little I won't notice. Then you take another, and then you think, maybe you better finish it all so maybe I won't remember. And then, before I get back, mother comes home and gives you something to eat. And sometimes even dad comes home and you eat with him."

"I like to eat with him."

"I know, Mel. But you better watch out. Someday you'll eat so much, no one will sit near you. You'll get as fat as he is. You'll fly away."

"That's not a true story, it's silly."

"If you don't go on a diet, it'll be true all right."

"You don't fly away if you get fatter, you just stay on the ground."

"Not if you're like a balloon, then you just fly away."

He went to his room and sat down at the desk staring out the window, not seeing anything outside. *She says she knows it all*, he thought. *But what does she know? She'll never know. I won't let her or anyone know.* Now looking out the window, craning his neck, he could make out a portion of the street. It was snowing and no one was there. All the children all over the world were laughing with their families, playing with their toys. But his parents were working, and his sister was getting ready to go ice-skating with some friends.

He opened a desk drawer and began to cram the little book inside. "I won't read it, he said. I won't." Then he heard the wind rattle the window and watched the snow swirl and swirl. He turned the pages of the book. "It's getting worse," he whispered, fanning the pages back and forth. "No. It shouldn't. No. But it is. It's getting worse. No!"

2.

It seemed to start that day in early December with the giggles of the boys in gym class. Mr. Wolfson was holding elimination races, and Mel and Sheldon were the last two left. Both boys got down on all fours, Wolfson blew the whistle, and they charged across the gym. As he ran panting along, he heard the laughing rise in his ears.

"Look at them! Look!" cried the boys. Already tired, he ran as fast as he could. His legs dragged, he puffed and perspired. But he beat Sheldon across the line. The boys tittered and laughed and cheered, "Hooray!"

"Yessir!" cried Mr. Wolfson. "They may not be the fastest, but they sure are the fattest," he said, bobbing his head and exchanging warm glances with the boys as they laughed and laughed.

Sheldon laughed too. But not Mel. So, all the laughter fell on him.

"He's fatter than you are, Mel," said his friend Murray, keeping his face straight. "You're real you're real plump, but he's the fattest one I ever saw."

"Yeah, but he can take it," said Johnny. "Sheldon can laugh but look at Mel!" And the laughter broke out again.

"Men! Men!" Mr. Wolfson admonished. "That's enough. The boys ran a good race. If they keep at it, they'll lose all that baby fat."

But they forgot the good race and remembered the fat. They remembered Mel's fat legs and his puffing. And they remembered his angry eyes. How those eyes had set them off! His winning told against him. Sheldon sank into the background, but not Mel.

In class Johnny put tacks on his chair and passed notes saying, "Mel is fat."

Walking home across the school park, Mel and Murray were followed by Johnny's gang. "Fatso! Fatso!"

"Leave him alone," said Murray.

"Why do you stick up for him, Murray? You're not fat," said Johnny.

"Just leave him alone."

"Fatso! Fatso!" cried the boys.

"Stop it!" Mel shouted.

"Stop being fat," said Billie.

"I'm not fat."

"No," said Johnny, "you're skinny. You're the skinniest kid in school. You know why you're so smart in class? You're fat. You've got a fat head."

"Don't listen to them," Murray advised. "Don't pay any attention and they'll get tired and leave you alone."

But he could not close his ears. He tried sometimes, even for days.

"Look at him," the boys jeered, "he's getting so fat he can't even talk." He sucked in his breath and held it. "He's blowing up blowing up!" they shouted.

"Like a dead fish," said Billie. He clenched his teeth and fists but still said nothing.

"Yeah, maybe he's dead," said Johnny. "Poke him, Billie. Go on."

"Hey fatso," said Billie. "Hey Piggy," he said, poking Mel.

"Stop it," said Murray.

"Maybe he's got his mouth stuffed with foo-ood!" said Johnny, pinching Mel's cheeks.

So Mel opened his mouth and shouted, "Stop that! Stop it!"

"Look," cried Billie, "what a fat mouth."

"Fatso!" they all cried, coming at him, poking at him. "Fatso! Piggy!"

"No!" he cried.

"Mel is fat! Mel is fat! Mel is fat!" they chanted.

So, it was no use. Each day the boys followed them. He and Murray tried to find new ways home, but the gang always found them out. Soon the December snows came, filling the school park and the street that ran along it to the big intersection at Town Street. and six, then eight, then ten boys lingered away from home and joined with Johnny. Then came Lois, one of the many new students who each day began arriving at the school after Thanksgiving break, and the first girl to join with Johnny.

"Mel is fat!" cried Lois.

"Mel is fat! Mel is fat!" they all cried, ranting and jeering all the way through the park to the Town Street crossing. Here the chants stopped short as the children came upon Officer Brown, who shuffled them off on their separate ways.

"It's just the leaders," Murray said one day. "If we could stop Johnny, the others would stop. I'll talk to him. He has nothing against me."

The last day before Christmas break, Johnny tripped Mel in the hall. Mel scrambled to his feet and raised his fist, but Murray pushed him aside. "Johnny, why don't you leave him alone? He doesn't bother you."

"I don't like fatsos," Johnny said. "And I don't like kids that can't take it."

"Why can't you find someone else to pick on? You've been after him long enough."

"Why can't you find someone else to walk home with?"

"He lives next door to me. He's my friend."

"Maybe you better make new friends. Why don't you walk home with me?"

"You don't live near me."

"You shouldn't walk home with him. We don't like it. Let him walk with Sheldon."

"He doesn't like Sheldon."

"But you like him," Johnny snarled. "Tell your fat friend to lose weight and then we'll stop. Even Mr. Wolfson says he's fat. Everyone says so, maybe you should say so too."

School let out early in the afternoon for the holidays. Mel and Murray hurried into the park with Susan, another new student, who had just started at the school that day.

"My mother said I should show her the way home," Murray explained.

"Maybe she should go alone," Mel said.

"I can't do that," said Susan.

"I've got to get her home," Murray said. "My mother said so."

Susan kept lingering behind, stopping, dawdling, looking here and there about the park. "I've never seen so much snow. Look at it fall."

"Come on," said Mel grimly.

"You better hurry, Susan," Murray said, taking her hand and dragging her along.

"Murray, I can't keep up. You're squeezing my hand!"

"See anything?" Murray asked. The wind sprayed snow in his eyes. "I can't see them." he said.

"See who?" asked Susan. "Why are we running, Murray? It's cold and mushy. Why don't we walk in the street like the other kids?"

"If we get to Town Street, we'll be all right," Murray said, puffing.

Mel tried to see the intersection. But they had wandered into a curving chain of high drifts. They couldn't see beyond the walls of snow. The wind whined and murmured. Town Street was far, far away, and they were already tired.

"I can't run anymore," said Susan.

"Maybe we can beat them," he said.

"If we can get over the snow, we " Suddenly he heard something whiz past his head. He glared at Murray.

"Why are we running?" asked Susan.

"Don't stop now," Murray pleaded, pulling her forward.

"Murray please!"

"Is it them?" asked Mel. The wind now seemed mixed with a low murmur of laughter, which grew louder and louder.

"What is it?" Susan asked. "What's wrong?" A snowball hit him on the left side. He turned toward the left and was hit on his right and in the face."

"They beat us for sure," said Murray. "They're in front too."

"Ow!" cried Susan. Snowballs came from all sides. "Ow!" she cried, hit again.

"Duck down!" Murray shouted, and the three clung close to the snow.

First arms, then capped heads appeared over the snowheaps. The air filled with snowballs.

"Why are they throwing them? Who are they?"

Voices rang out: "Merry Christmas, Santa Claus! Fatso! Fatso!"

Susan stared suddenly at Mel. "Ah-h!" she shrieked, hit again. She began to cry.

Mel made a snowball and cocked his arm.

"Mel! Don't do it!" shouted Murray. "They'll only throw more. ... Mel!"

But the snowball went flying. "Fatso can't take it! Fatso can't take it!"

The snowballs came faster. One hit Murray in the face. He reached down and made a snowball of his own. "Fat and Skinny! Mutt and Jeff!"

"Look out, Murray!" warned Mel. But they hit Murray again and again.

"Why are they hitting us?" Susan whimpered. "We didn't hurt them. It isn't fair."

"I'm sorry," Mel said. He grasped the snow in his frozen hands. He threw wildly again and again. He had no time to pack them, they split in mid-air.

"It won't work," said Murray. "We'll have to run past them."

"We'll get hurt," said Susan.

"If we get to the street, we can run to Town Avenue," said Mel.

"They'll hurt us."

"What else can we do, Susan?" said Murray. He took her by the hand and ran toward the street that paralleled the park and led to the intersection.

Mel stood straight up and glared at the snow piles. The voices echoed, "Ya! Ya! Fatso! Ya! Ya!"

And more snowballs went crashing his way. He shielded his face, sidestepped, but was hit again and again. "I hate you all!" he shouted.

"Hurry up, Mel!" Murray called, and Mel scampered after him.

They could not see the street for the snow piles. But they made their way, followed by the snowballs and the jeering voices. "Fat and Skinny," the voices chanted. "Mutt and Jeff!" "Stan and Ollie!"

"I can't see the street," Susan said. "I can't see anything."

"Quick ... over the hill," Murray said, pulling her up the high icy pilings.

As they reached the top, the snowballs hit again. Susan and Murray bounded out of sight. Mel took a last look down on the field.

"Look out, Fatso!" they called. "We can't miss you." They pelted him again, moving closer, closer. "Run, Fatso! Let's see Fatso run!" He gasped and wheezed in helpless rage as they hit him over and over. Then he started running, scrambling over the hill and skidding down the other side.

"Come on! Hurry!" Murray yelled. "You're so slow, Mel. Look! Come on! There's the corner! There's the policeman!"

He ran after them down the slushy street, hearing his feet splash and his chest pant and heave.

"Fatso! Look at Fatso go!" they called. Icy snowballs flew past him, splashing in slush, splattering against the street. "We'll get you again," one voice cried, "we'll get you every day after Christmas!"

And one last wet and cold snowball landed on the back of his neck.

Susan and Murray slowed to a walk. He came up to them as they neared the corner, where Officer Brown waited to lead them across the street.

"Hi kids," said the policeman, "A little late today, huh? Don't think I don't know what you've been up to," he said, smiling and winking at them as they reached the far corner. "You kids!" he said.

They walked on in silence, breathing hard, unwilling to speak or look at each other, kicking the slush before them.

"They hit us because you're fat, didn't they?" Susan asked finally.

"I'm sorry, Susan. I said you should go alone."

"And Murray," she continued. "Why did they call you skinny?... Murray! What's wrong?... Murray, your nose is bleeding!"

"I got it from the first hit. When they called me skinny."

"Does it hurt?" she asked.

"It's real sore. I'll have to lie about it at home."

"Why? Why don't you tell them what happened? Mel, why don't you tell your parents?"

He reached down and made a snowball. He smashed it against a tree trunk.

"What're you going to do? They'll chase you again. They'll beat you up."

Murray made a snowball and threw it against the same tree.

"I'm sorry," Mel repeated angrily.

Murray put his hand to his nose again. "Maybe you better lose some weight." He walked faster, dragging Susan with him. Mel kept pace, he stared down at the dirty slush.

"It'll be alright after Christmas. ... We have ten days off. Maybe they'll forget about it."

"Maybe," Murray muttered.

"You know what?" said Susan, as they reached Mel's house. "I don't think you're fat, Mel. I didn't even think about it before they said it."

Mel took her hand and squeezed it lightly. He half-smiled. "Maybe things will change," he said.

3.

On the night of Christmas Day, mother and father came home early. Mother slipped on an apron and started setting the table. Elaine helped, while he and father watched.

"Only ten o'clock," said Elaine. "Must've been a rough one."

"We were short help," said mother.

"But we sure did the business," said father. "Lines of people waiting what lines!"

"He gave them too much, he overstocked again," said mother. "Look at all this food, Elaine. And there's plenty where this came from, believe me."

"You can never tell what's going to happen," said father. "They expect a little more on a holiday, and what if you don't have it—you can't let them down at Christmas."

"All I know is we work day and night, and for what?"

Mel winced. Mother always found ways to hurt. Her face is always long, she's always tired, always complaining or yelling. He wanted to know why. What was wrong? What was wrong with him and father?

Father put down his magazine and opened a bag. "I almost forgot, Mel. I brought home some extra goodies for you." And he handed some small cartons to mother.

Father was a stranger who lived in the house, hardly ever there. But Mel was always happy to see him, until mother or Elaine ruined it. They always did.

"Extra food again? That's all he needs. You always bring home treats and he always eats them."

Mother slammed a platter of turkey sandwiches on the table. "That's the least we can do is see he has enough to eat," she said, glaring at father.

"Good food too, right, Mel?" said Father, squeezing his shoulder.

"Enough to eat!" squealed Elaine. "You don't know what happens here. Don't you see how fat he's getting?"

"Since when do you take such an interest in your brother? You're always running off at the drop of a hat."

"Don't pick on me because you're too busy to be with him."

"I suppose I should never leave the house," mother returned. "Is that what you want?"

"All right, stop it," said father. "Right now things are a little tight..."

"His pants are tight."

"Your mother and I have to work, and you'll have to make the best of it."

"You're spoiling him, you do too much for him."

"Why shouldn't we do all we can?"

He couldn't get his sandwich down, but father was having no trouble. Between bites, he smiled at Mel, and Mel tried to smile back. The two women turned hard angry eyes on father. They hate him, he thought. Why do they hate him? How can he be so calm when they ? What's wrong with him? What's he done?

"Look how much Daddy's eating." said Elaine. "That's why Mel eats so much."

"Don't you think you've had enough?" mother ask father.

"Just having a snack…"

"Oh it's easy for you to make jokes, for you to smile and eat your fill. Trying to be the big man just because your friends got big. Working our lives away in the restaurant just to look big."

"And you are big all right," said Elaine. "Like a balloon!"

"Elaine!" father said softly.

"Want to end up like daddy?" his sister asked him. "You'll fly away," she whispered in his ear.

"Well, it's true, he's putting on weight, just like you," said mother.

"I have to sample the food, don't I?" father said.

"I've had enough of your jokes," said mother. "We've heard them all: the big funny restaurant man, as big in size like his friends are in money. ..."

"Oh come on."

"You can tell jokes, that's your business. But now you've dragged all of us into it. I have to keep after him all the time, Elaine.

Throwing away money just to look big, and each day we're getting poorer. I have to follow him around just to keep him in line."

"Please," said father.

"I'm tired of following, that's all. Look, look at me, see how old I'm getting. And look at him so pink and happy."

For the first time he saw the deep lines on her face, the wrinkles around her eyes, the droop of her mouth at rest.

"Please," said father. "Not in front of the boy."

"You're the big man, aren't you? You're so thoughtful. They don't see you the way I do. You wear me out and I then I have to cope with them. I don't like my children to see me like this, but what can I do about it? I'm the one who has to yell at them. Haven't we punished them enough?" She began sobbing. "Just so you can be the big man."

"Mother, don't cry, mother," said Elaine, crying with her.

He began crying too, still not understanding fully. Father was the stranger, who was kind and full of jokes, always good, always kind and calm whenever he saw him, no matter how things were. But now he just sat there, and Mel began to understand the secret. Father looked so helpless, brooding across the table, looking at the others with dull, tired eyes floating in a sea of flesh. He's calm because there's nothing he can do. He's fat. And then he realized that father was not calm at all. Beneath his paunch were a pain and rage so terrible, he didn't dare let them out the pain and rage of those who are fat. Yes, he is fat, Mel thought. He has that restaurant, he works, he stays away. That's why he's fat and that's why they hate him.

They sat in silence, playing with their food, none of them really eating. Father patted his arm, but he squirmed away.

"Well, this is one beautiful night" said father.

Mother raised her head and pushed the hair away from her eyes. "I guess we'll have to make the best of it after all."

"Tell him about the surprise," father said eagerly.

Mel looked from face to face.

"Well, what happens next week, Mel?" asked mother.

"It's your birthday, stupid," said Elaine. "Don't tell me you can't remember."

"You'll be " father began, and then stopped.

"He'll be ten," said mother.

"You're going to have a party, son. We've invited all your classmates "

"All...my..."

"Not all," said mother. "It's a small party."

"Just before school," said Elaine.

"All right, not all," said father. "Just the important ones."

"Just show him the list," said mother.

Father drew out his wallet and took a slip of paper from it, handing the slip to Mel. First on the list were Murray and Susan, then Lois, Billie, Johnny...

"You don't look very excited," said Elaine.

"He will be," said father, "when he sees the presents ... and the games we've planned...We're supplying all the food, the best "

"You never had a party before," he said.

"This year is different," said mother.

"You always said it was too soon after Christmas."."

"Well, they can give him some of their extra gifts."

He looked at his mother and father, then back at the list.

"What's wrong, Mel?"

"You didn't even ask him if he wanted all those kids," said Elaine.

"We wanted to surprise him," father said.

"And now you've told him."

"I won't be there. I wanted to see the look on his face."

"Well, look. ... Maybe he doesn't like those kids."

"Sure he does," said father.

"Sure," Elaine sneered. "He loves all of them."

"Why why did you invite Johnny?" he asked.

"Johnny's mother's a friend of ours, Mel. Don't you like Johnny?"

"I don't want a party. They'll laugh at me."

"You're having a party," she said sharply. "Every one's invited already."

"Take it easy," said father.

"Well I never heard such a thing. We try to make it up to the boy "

"You try too hard, mother," said Elaine. "It only makes it worse."

"It's the way you do it," said father.

"The way I do it! This was your idea. You get all the ideas and I have to carry them out."

"All right," said father. "So we don't have a party. Is that what you want, Mel?"

For a moment he brightened. "I "

"Your mother will just have to call all the children and tell them we can't have a party after all."

He looked down at his plate, at his half-eaten sandwich. "If you don't want a party, that's all right by us. I guess we shouldn't try so hard for you. I guess we should let you go your own way."

"All right ... all right," he muttered.

"See how grateful he is," said Elaine.

"I knew you'd understand, son. Maybe I should've asked you before, but I wanted to surprise you. We can't turn around and tell everyone not to come, can we? That wouldn't be right..."

"No..."

"Besides, you'll have a swell time, you'll see. You'll have the best fixings ever: Sandwiches, cake. I'll have our baker "

"All right!" he cried. "All right!" And without looking back, he ran to his room.

4.

On the night before his birthday, he dreamed that a large ball of snow rolled across the windy field getting bigger and bigger. Linda and Murray ran from it, swiftly rolling a ball of their own. Only theirs was black.

"Hello!" he called, trying to raise his voice above the wind. Linda waved her hand, but Murray kept pushing the ball.

"Come on, Linda!" Murray called.

"But Murray," she answered.

"Murray!" he shouted. Murray pushed the ball aside, took Linda by the hand and stalked off the field. Linda waved frantically as Murray dragged her away. *He will be tall*, he thought as the wind died. *He'll smoke a pipe just like his father*.

"Mmm," said a man's voice.

"Mmm," said Murray's voice. Murray and his father, dressed the same, sat in identical chairs smoking identical pipes. M, dressed like an orchestra conductor, snapped the stem of a pipe in two.

"Bravo!" thousands cheered, clapping their hands.

M bowed and Linda begged: "Marry me."

"I'll consider it," he said.

"Please!" she pleaded, kneeling before him. "Please! Please!"

"Rise, Linda," he said with compassion. "I will marry you since you asked me to do so. You are not perfect. But I will teach you in time."

Water lapped against the ship, wind filled the mast, as they sailed away, she so pretty in her flowing gown, her head upon his shoulder as he steered toward the setting sun. But then when she drew back and smiled, it was not Mel who, with proud, loving eyes, turned from the helm to her. "Murray!" she cried with joy.

The wind howled. "It's coming! It's coming!" he shouted in panic.

The black ball rolled toward him faster, getting bigger, getting faster, bigger huge ... crashing against the bowling pins!

And now his stomach grew and grew and grew a mouth that talked to him. "Mm, that was good," said the stomach in a voice that was high-pitched and wheedling, cheerful, yet insistent, all at once. "Mm, yes, I want more."

Thousands of children watched him and laughed as he sat on a stage surrounded by heaps of food, stacks and stacks of meats and pies and cakes. Helplessly he stuffed himself, as the laughter grew louder and his stomach demanded: "Yes more. Mm... more. Give me more. I won't ever stop."

"No," said M, stuffing his mouth.

"Eat I say. You wouldn't want to make me die. If I die, you die. So eat. Fill me up. Make me grow."

Trucks roared along the highways blowing their horns; airplanes zoomed by in formation; trains from all points made their way to the stage where he sat.

"Eat, eat," said his stomach over and over again. "More," it said, "more," while the children and now the adults all the people of the world clapped their hands in rhythm and chanted, "Look at him go, see him go!"

By truck, by plane, by train the food poured in. Begging hands, brown, black, yellow and white, reached out, but the food went into the stacks and heaps beyond the hungry and angry people. The stacks of food grew, and so did his stomach.

"My goodness," said the people. "My goodness, he's gone," they said, their voices fading away.

"Please," he whispered, "Please."

And then the stomach, the people disappeared. Father and Mother hovered over him as he continued to eat.

"Grr," growled Mother.

"Grr," growled Father.

They growled at each other in hatred, then smiled sweetly down on him. "Our boy," they simpered.

Mother's tired face grew older and older. Father grew younger, slimmer. His eyes slanted up, his hair turned red. And on his head, he sprouted two horns. "You wouldn't want us to stop, would you, M? Ha! Ha! Ha!"

And now father's laughter merged with the laughter of the boys and girls, with their rhythmic handclapping and their chanting. "Mel is fat, Mel is fat," they chanted.

They formed a circle in his living room, laughing, chanting and clapping their hands, linking their arms, Linda and Murray now with them, and other, new boys and girls with strangely twisted and blurred faces moving around in a circle that ever grew tighter and smaller. The floor was covered with shattered dishes and toys. The party table was overturned. Sandwiches lay in red pools of punch. And amid the wreckage he sat, crying wildly, licking punch-stained icing off huge pieces of birthday cake. The children sang, laughing louder and circling around him, but it was not the usual song:

Happy birthday,
Happy happy birthday,
This is your day,
But we have all the fun.

Their singing and laughter rose to a roar, as they spun faster and faster around him. And in the din, familiar voices blurted out, spurring the laughter on.

"You kids," said Officer Brown.

"You'll fly away," said Fran.

"Men, men!" said Mr. Wolfson.

"Mmm," said Murray's father.

"Mmm," said Murray.

"Grr," said mother.

"Grr," said father.

"If I die, you die," said the stomach.

"No, no ... No!" he shouted, sitting up in bed. "It's not my party. It's a little boy's someplace else. I'm not invited." But the party was his and he knew it. "All right...all right. It's going to happen. Well, let it...let it!"

And now, moved by the force of dreams, he knew what he must do.

5.

They gathered in the living room, sitting primly in their seats, looking shy, guilty almost. They followed his movements, afraid to speak, waiting, until finally his mother spoke.

"Mel, why didn't you show them the game your father bought? ... Pin the tail—"

"Ah," said Johnny almost sneering, "we play that all the time."

"Not with a prize like this," said mother, taking a package off the table. It was wrapped in green paper with a red ribbon. She shook it seductively.

"What is it?" asked Lois.

"Don't worry, you'll see. Now you children play while I get the refreshments ready. You've never seen such a spread," Johnny began to laugh.

"What's so funny?" mother asked.

"Let's play," said Mel.

"Mel, stop looking so mopey," she said. "He's so mopey these days, you'd think he didn't want a party."

"Let's play!" he said.

"Let's eat!" said Billie.

"Yes...yes...in a little while," she said, retreating to the kitchen.

"She's funny," said Lois. "She's so fidgety."

"That's 'cause she works," said Billie. "My mother doesn't work, does yours?" "No," said Lois. "She says that's not nice."

"That's why I'm so funny," Mel said. The children stared.

"Let's play," said Susan.

"All right, Susan," he said. "Here's the blindfold. Girls first."

Susan, then Lois, then Murray took their turns. They were spun around and then set free. They tripped and bumped into furniture. At last they found the donkey on the wall, stabbing him in the eye, in the leg. Murray hit the white space. Then Johnny took his turn and pinned the tail low on the donkey's rump.

"You win, Johnny," said Lois. "That was real good."

"I haven't gone yet," said Billie.

"Neither have I," said Mel.

"Hey! Gimme that blindfold," Billie said.

"That's not fair, Mel," said Susan. "You should go last."

"It's my party."

"That's why it's not fair."

"What's fair's fair," said Murray. "Susan's right."

He glared at Murray, fastened the blindfold, and spun himself round and round. Johnny grabbed his arm and spun him faster, pushing him toward the wall away from the donkey. He groped along the wall, trying to find the sheet of paper.

"You're getting warm," said Johnny. But he reached out his hand and touched the door trim.

"You're lying," he said. He made his way to the adjacent wall, carefully skirting a chair.

"That's not fair," said Billie. "He knows the room."

"That's all right, Billie. Let him go," said Murray.

The table is next, he told himself. He raised his hand higher to avoid knocking pictures and knick-knacks off the tier table.

"Johnny!" Murray exclaimed. But it was too late. Johnny jarred him against the table, as he and some objects tumbled to the floor. The children scurried away from the mess.

"Look!" said Billie.

"Let me see," said Lois. "Ooh is he fat!"

"Like father like son," Johnny snarled, just above a whisper.

Mel ripped off the blindfold and stared into the leering faces of Johnny and Billie. He turned his head and saw Murray whispering in Susan's ear. Susan saw him first and nudged Murray. They frowned at him guiltily. In Susan's hand was the picture of him with his father.

"You're fat like your old man," said Billie.

"You're so fat, you couldn't win," said Johnny.

"I had it won if you didn't trip me." Mel insisted.

"You shouldn't even try to win at your own party," said Lois.

"He's fat," said Johnny. "He wants everything."

"That's right," he answered. "I want all I can get. It's my birthday and I should win."

"Children!" mother said. She ran into the room, wiping her hands on her apron. They turned to her as she looked at the pictures scattered on the floor.

"Johnny won and Mel says he won," said Lois. "He didn't win, and he knocked over all those pictures."

"Mel, shame on you," said mother. "You shouldn't even try to win."

"I don't care."

"Here, Mel," she said, handing him the prize. "Give it to Johnny."

"I "

"Give it to Johnny."

He held his breath and handed over the package. "Thank you," said Johnny.

"Now let's have no more of this," said mother. "Let's go into the kitchen and have something to eat. Mel, pick up the pictures."

Giggling and whispering, they followed mother into the kitchen. Susan and Murray stopped at the door and looked back at him, but he turned away. When they were gone, he stooped down and lifted the father-son picture. There was his father standing in front of a banquet spread, a fat man with his arm on the shoulder of his fat son. A diagonal crack in the glass sliced the picture in half.

"Ooh!" they exclaimed in the kitchen.

"Mel's father made this. We own a restaurant," mother said.

It's happening, he thought. It's happening and I don't care.

"Mel!" mother called. He placed the picture on the table, facedown. And, drawing a deep breath, he marched into the kitchen.

"Don't stuff yourselves," said mother, as they devoured the food she served. "Save room for the cake."

Wearing glossy New Year's party hats, they sat around the table, eating from platters filled with cocktail sandwiches of tuna, salami, and cream cheese and jelly, drinking from cups brimming with red punch.

"There's so much here, we'll never eat it all," said Lois.

"Just do your best. Mel's father didn't want you to go away hungry. Mel, why don't you put on your hat?"

"I don't want to," and he began to stuff sandwich after sandwich into his craw.

"Stop stuffing yourself, Mel. What are you trying to do?"

"Eat," he mumbled, his mouth fully stuffed. "Eat as much as I can."

They began to laugh.

"This isn't funny," said mother. "You eat too much as it is."

"He's too fat, isn't he?" asked Johnny.

"Mel! Pick up your hat! Why are you acting this way?"

He answered by gobbling another sandwich.

"Stop eating, Mel. Pick up your hat this instant."

"He's a bad kid," said Billie. "Just like Johnny says."

"He certainly is," said mother. "And if he doesn't stop, he'll have his father to deal with. Mel, if you don't stop, I'll send the children home."

But he wouldn't stop. He reached both hands across the table, snaring bits of food at random, reaching again as soon as the food was packed in his mouth. "Send them home," he said. "Then I'll have more to eat."

"I've never seen you this way, Mel."

"Maybe you better bring the cake," said Susan. "Then he'll have to stop."

"Yes, Susan. That's a good idea." She crossed to the pantry, opened the door, and, her hand on the doorknob, she turned and then opened the door and entered.

"See how sad you made her, Mel?" said Susan. "That's no way to act. After she's gone to all this trouble " He plucked a sandwich from her plate and swallowed it. "Mel!"

"Why don't you tell me I'm bad, Murray? That's what you want to do, and now you can."

"You see, Murray," said Johnny.

"You are bad. You're right," Murray said at last.

"Ooh!" Lois cried. Mother stood in front of the pantry door, holding a huge white cake with seven candles on it. "Happy birthday," they sang.

"How do you like that for a cake?" said mother proudly.

"Just right for me," he said. "I'll eat it all."

"No you won't," said mother. "You'll have no more than anyone else, I'll see to that. Everyone will take some cake home with them."

"No they won't," he said.

"Now listen here, Mel. Everyone will get the same amount. I'm going to cut this cake, and when I do, I don't want to hear another word, not one word. You don't deserve all this as it is."

"What's that sticking out of the cake?" asked Billie.

"It looks like a penny," said Lois.

"That's right," said mother. "This is a special cake a money cake. Mel's father had it filled with coins, with nickels, dimes, quarters, pennies. There's even a half a dollar for the lucky one."

"Ooh, money's dirty," said Susan.

"No, Susan, they're boiled in water, they're all clean as a whistle."

"Whistles are dirty," said Johnny.

Billie laughed, "Only fat ones."

"We keep all the money?" asked Lois.

"Of course you do."

"I'll get the most," said Mel.

"You get what you get," said mother.

"I want the silver dollar," he said.

"It's a half dollar, hog," said Billie.

"In one minute, you'll get nothing, understand?"

"Light the candles."

Mother struck a match and lit the candles one by one. "There," she said. "Now, make a wish, Mel, and blow them out."

He stood up and closed his eyes. And with all his might he made his wish. *I wish I get the biggest piece with the most money,* he wished. *I wish they get almost nothing and beg me for a penny.* Then he leaned over the cake and blew as hard as he could.

"You got them all," said mother. "Now take a knife and make the first cut... From the middle that's it. Now let me take over."

"I want the biggest piece," he said.

"For once in your life, you'll get the same as everyone else," she said, carefully cutting even slices. "Here, Susan, Johnny..."

"That's not big enough," he said when he received his share. "It's not as big as Billie's."

"That's all you're getting," said mother.

"I have a dime and a quarter," said Johnny.

"Three pennies and a nickel," said Billie.

"Children, don't chop up your cake, you're making a mess."

"Who has the half dollar?" he asked. "Murray, do you ?" Murray nodded and held up a shiny half dollar.

"It's not right," Mel said. "I only got a nickel."

"Now, Mel, stop pouting," said mother. "Eat your cake like everyone else." He reached across the table and grabbed another piece.

"Mel!" she screamed and slapped him. "There. I told you you couldn't have any more. You've asked for that all afternoon."

"I don't care," he said.

"On your birthday," she said.

"Give me the cake. Why should Murray have the most?"

"He's real bad," said Billie. "He's spoiled."

"I want the cake. I should have the most."

"Well, you're not getting any more," said mother. "I've coddled you enough."

"You hate me, that's why. You gave them more on purpose. And they hate me. You all hate me."

"Mel, I'm warning you for the last time. If you carry on, I'll send the children home and their presents with them."

"Let them have their presents, see if I care."

He lunged at the cake and threw it on the floor.

"Mel!" Susan cried.

"He's bad," said Johnny. "He should be get it."

"That's all," mother said, her voice full of anger. "That's all I can bear."

"Send them home," he said. "I don't want you here, I hate all of you."

"I've got two quarters," Johnny whispered to him. And with that, Mel pushed his hands against the table, lifting it with all his might, as he leaned back on his chair and toppled it to the floor. The cups of punch fell over; the punch bowl slid off the table and crashed to the floor. The children jumped from their seats.

"Send them home," he said sobbing wildly. "Then I'll eat everything."

"Look at him," said Lois, astonished.

"All right, children. I'm sorry," said mother. "Pick up your coins."

"Mel's bad, isn't he?" asked Murray.

"He's worse than that, Murray," said mother. "Don't worry, it's not your fault... All of you, come on. Out of the kitchen."

They moved to the other room, their voices getting further and further away.

"You'll have to go home," he heard mother say. "Here, let me give you back your presents."

"Do we have to do that?"

"I'm sorry, Susan, he's got to learn."

He heard them move into the front parlor, heard mother helping them on with their coats. For an instant, he thought of calling, begging them to come back. But then, he felt a kind of darkness fill him, he could not speak nor think nor hear at all. Finally, mother's footsteps sounded louder and louder, until she entered the kitchen. She tried to put away some dishes, but then sat down, sighing and breathing deeply. The only sounds were their breathing and punch drip-dropping off the table.

"Mel, Mel," she sobbed. How could you do a thing like this after all we did? ... They'll go home to their parents and tell them. They'll say I don't know how to raise you."

"You don't care about me," he said, all his bitterness returning.

"Not care about you... Just let your father hear that when he gets home. Just let him hear what his wonderful son did today."

"Tell him," he said. "Let him beat me with his strap."

"All right," she said. "That's just what he'll do."

"Let him," he said with terror and pleasure. "Let him!"

6.

He managed to get through the first day of school, and when the final bell rang, he broke from the lines of children and hurried onto School Street. The wind whistled, and only after walking for some time did he realize that Susan and Murray were just a few steps behind him.

"Well?" he said, stopping and glaring at them.

"Don't do it, Murray," he heard Susan say.

"Come on," Murray answered, "I've got to."

"You don't want him to walk with me, do you, Susan?"

"It isn't that, Mel, he "

"I thought I should tell you, Mel," said Murray. "I can't walk home with you anymore."

"I knew you'd say that."

"It's not what you think," Murray said. "My mother told me not to walk home with you. She didn't like me getting hurt."

"That's a lie," he said.

"No it's not."

"I told him not to listen to her, Mel. But he can't. She's his mother."

"Why are you walking with me now? I didn't ask you to."

"I wanted to tell you," said Murray.

"I don't want to walk with you. I want to walk by myself." He started walking again. Murray and Susan followed him.

"Mel, you make the kids hurt you," said Susan.

"It's none of your business what I do. You're not my friend."

"But Mel "

"There he is!" a voice cried out. He looked around and saw Johnny and Billie and other children running toward him.

"Don't look at me," said Murray. "I didn't know."

"What are we going to do?" Susan asked.

He put his hands on his hips, took a deep breath, and moved a few paces toward the children.

"You can't run away this time," said Billie, coming up to him.

"No, I can't run like you," he answered. "I'm too fat to run. Besides, I don't have to run."

"You're fat all right," said Johnny. "Fat like your old man."

"I'm not fat like him. I'm fat like no one else."

"My mother says your restaurant's no good," said Lois. "That's why you're fat," she says. "She says only a real bad boy would do what you did."

"Can't you leave him alone?" said Susan.

"I thought you and your girl weren't going to walk with him, Skinny," said Johnny.

"He's not walking with me. He's on your side and so's she. You're all skinny," he said. "I'm better than you."

"You're fat," said Billie. "You're a bad kid."

"Fatsos are better. They're stronger."

"Oh yeah?" said Billie.

"Hey Shannon, you hear that?"

"Oh yeah," said a tall boy with a sneering face, coming up to the children with a group of his own.

"Who's this, Billie?"

"My cousin Shannon's who. And all his friends," said Billie. "He's in the fifth grade. I told him what you did."

"You think fat kids are stronger, fatso?" said Shannon.

"Don't answer him, Mel," said Susan. "He's too big."

"They they live longer," he said. "Skinny people don't eat enough...You'll all die before me. And Murray first."

"Mel!" Susan cried.

"It's true," he howled bitterly. "Fat kids are stronger. I can beat you all up."

"Don't let him say that, Shan," said a scrawny friend of Shannon. "Show these little kids."

Mel backed toward the snow drifts on the curb. "I'm not afraid of you," he said. "You're all fakes."

"Hit him, Shannon," the children cried. "Hit 'im in the belly."

"I'll show you...I'll show you I'm not afraid," said Mel.

"Says you," said Shannon, cocking his arm and moving toward him.

He shoved Mel against the snow drift. Top snow fell on Mel's head, and his enemies laughed. He wiped the snow from his eyes and moved to the other side of a trash can across from Shannon. A large crowd of children gathered now. He saw them laughing and biting their lower lips with excitement. He began stalking Shannon around the trash can, cocking his fist. Shannon backed away, with mock fear.

"You still think you're stronger, Fatso? You think you can beat me up?"

"Look at Mel, Shannon," said Billie. "He's shaking. He's chicken. He's a fat chicken. He won't fight."

"Hit "im anyway," said Shannon's scrawny friend. "Hit "im in the belly."

"Naw," said Shannon, mocking. "You think I really should?"

"Don't fight, Mel," said Susan. "They'll all know now."

"Fatso! Fatso! Chicken!" shouted the children.

"Hey!" Shannon cried.

Mel sprang at him and knocked him over the trash can. He grabbed his arms and yanked him into the snow drift.

"Come on, Shannon! Hit him! Get him!" Shannon tried to push Mel off, but the snow gave, and he sank deeper into the drift.

"He's too heavy for 'im! He can't get up!" Lois cried.

Mel let off some pressure and Shannon pushed him away, standing up.

"Now I'll show you," Shannon said, panting. But Mel rushed him and they both fell down. Over and over they rolled, but Mel landed on top and pressed Shannon's arms into the slushy street.

"Get up! Get up, Shannon!" the children cried. Shannon twisted and turned but he couldn't get up.

"Give up," said Mel.

"Say I'm stronger."

"Get off me!" Shannon squealed.

"Not till you say I'm stronger. Say it!" He held his breath, waiting for some word, some sign from the others.

"Let him up, fatso," said Billie.

"Not till he says I'm stronger."

"You're not stronger, you're fatter," said Johnny. But the only sign was a snowball that thumped against his back. And now they pelted him with snowballs. They scooped up the spilt garbage and hurled oranges and bananas, empty milk cartons. He began crying, smashing Shannon's hands against the icy asphalt again and again.

"Ow! Ow!" cried Shannon. "Help me!"

"Give up," Mel chanted madly. "Give up! Give up!"

"Look out, Mel!" Susan cried. Shannon's friend rushed forward and clutched at Mel's arms. Murray ran over and tried to pull the friend off.

"Let him go!" said Murray. "He won."

Shannon's friend pulled Mel off and squared for a fight. But Mel pushed him away and clutched at Murray.

"Look out Murray!" called Susan.

"I don't need you!" said Mel, wrestling Murray to the ground. "I don't need your help."

"I know," said Murray. "Ow! I know!"

"Here comes the cop!" said Billie.

Officer Brown pushed the children left and right. "Okay, you kids. Break it up. ... You, Mel, get up. ... Mel!"

He loosened his hold and stood up. Murray rolled over and scrambled to his feet.

"Mel started it," said Johnny.

"I saw it all," said Officer Brown. "I've had my eyes open for some time. I'm surprised, Mel, real surprised. You fighting and with Murray."

"You should see what he did yesterday," said Lois.

"I can guess," said Officer Brown. "Now you Mel!"

He broke from the children and climbed up on the high snow pile, out of the grasp of everyone.

"I'm gonna report this," warned Officer Brown as the wind began to rise.

"I don't care what you do," he answered.

"Now you get down from there. You get down."

But he climbed higher and higher, and entered the snow-filled park.

"Mel!" Susan cried mournfully, her voice now far away. "They'll all know now the whole school...everyone!"

"Want to come with me?" he dared her.

"I can't, Mel," she called. "I have to go with Murray. My mother "

"Then I'm glad," he said. "Let the whole school know. Tell my folks. Tell everyone. I'm better than all of you."

"Come back, Mel!" Officer Brown called. The wind whined and whistled, the children raised their arms toward him.

"Fatso! Fatso!" they called, their voices rising above the wind.

He looked down at them, clustered around the policemen, in silhouette against the snow. There was Murray and Susan and Lois and Officer Brown himself, and Johnny and Billie and Shannon and all Shannon's friends. And others a multitude of others all together, arm in arm, all against him, forever.

"I'm stronger and fatter," he called. "And I'll stay fat. Even if I get thin, I'll still be fat. I won't change for any of you!"

The wind rose, and again they raised their arms and waved. Their lips moved, forming words of derision. But they were tiny now, and their voices were faint and far away.

Valentine's Day

1.

The door reflects dull hall light. He turns key and knob, then draws back hands, flexing them, thrusting the cold out along his fingers—the outside cold, away. From a pocket he takes the crumpled letter:

To Susan

He breaks the seal, tugs to free the card, cracking a bond of paste. Thick red-paper heart—lopsided, ragged: deep pencil-scars crisscross around the edge —here, there; in the center, dry bubbles of paste seep out through holes in a white paper doily, and below, in black on the red:

Love Mel

He yanks the light cord. In the dark his breath comes short and loud. He yanks again. The cord trembles, the string weight ticks from wall to wall. Cramming heart and envelope into his pocket, he opens the door and steps inside. Pivoting, he kicks some last snowflakes at the floor mat, slams the door and calls:

"Ee-laine! Are you home? Ee-laine!"

2.

Under the window, dirty unscraped dishes and pots crowd the drainboard and peer over the rim of the sinkwell. Below, on the floor, a box brimming with garbage, a column of ants invading, parading on the brown table, amid the bread and cake crumbs, the spilt sugar.

The clock is yellow, a blur almost. Outside the window, it is grey flecked with white… *It's late.* He undoes his coat, flings it on a chair, then stands perfectly still. Faucet drips carom off water-filled plates, the clock whirrs... No other sound... except a low murmur from the stove. Vapor rises from two black pots. On the stove-tray, a red and white tin can — a tin-can, big-hatted chef smiles and holds out a platter of spaghetti... *She is home.*

He takes up his coat and hangs it on the hook, rushes out of the kitchen and down the dark, narrow corridor, past all the rooms and doors, into the living-room and then, turning off to the side, into her room: cold, cluttered, and loud with the grind and moan of cars and cars plodding through slush. "Come on, Ee-laine! Where are you?" *She's stepped out for a minute—or...* He swishes through the dresses and sweaters in the closet, crouches, and squints under chairs, under the bed, past the shoes and dust—even under father's desk.

"Come on, Ee—" He rises, his body rigid, tensed: *She's not fooling this time, she's dead! —or run far away — away... This dark house forever—with no one!...* Saying softly: "Elaine?"

He runs back along the corridor. "Elaine ... please!" He stops... A crackle — loud, *too loud: the turning of a page? ... Yes —of course!* Under the bathroom door, a seam of light. "Here you are Elaine. I found you." Another page turned, thundered. *Her games!* "You can't fool me, Elaine. You're in the bathroom. You're reading a magazine" Silence... a page. "Elaine, it's me-Mel!" *Not a game? ...No one home after all.... Or—maybe it's not her, but some murderer, some kidnapper.* "Please, Elaine, talk to me-please!" Another page. "You are here! It's you!" Silence. "It isn't fair... Why don't you talk to me? If you don't talk to me, I'll do something you won't like." Silence. He shakes the doorknob. Not a sound. "I'm warning you, Elaine. You better talk to me." He rattles the knob—louder, louder. "Elaine! The house is on fire! Ooh, it's terrible! Big red flames, Elaine! Big red flames.... Ooh—oh! They're coming closer! Ooh! I'm burning! Elaine! Save me! I'm burning—burning!" The flames leap up, scorch his skin, singe his hair.

Before him, the bathroom door; in his hand, the doorknob—free. He bounces it, then smashes it back into place — his voice shaking, pained: "Come on, Elaine, talk to me. Please talk to me!" Bracing up against the far wall, crashing into the door again, again. "You're not fair. I'll tell mother—that's what I'll do." He sobs wildly, spiraling down to the floor, his hands twisting the knob. "Why don't you talk to me? Why?"

A sharp tear of paper. He catches his sob and drops his arms, letting the knob click back. A plunge of water, a rustle of clothes, her shoes scuffle across the tiles. His fingers probe cracks in the dry, worn linoleum.

She is inches away now. He tenses his neck, rushes fists to his temples. The latch is turned, the door squeals open. His chin pressed against his chest, his knees against his stomach. He does not hear her footsteps and barely feels her skirt brush against him. Yet somehow knowing she has passed, he turns to see her... not walking, but almost marching—stiffly, evenly, not too fast—toward the kitchen, entering it, closing, and not even slamming, the kitchen door behind her.

Not even slamming the door! His eyes shut, his lips curve up. His face is taut crockery: it trembles, shatters and crumbles. He tries to stop the crying, muffles — the sound only. Tears streak his face, sting his cheeks. He tries to wipe them away but fails. The tears bring tears. *Let her cook dinner. Let her! I won't eat it. I'll never eat her food again. I won't. Never.*

He takes slow, deep breaths. Crying and breathing become one rhythm... slower... slower... Now there is silence, no sound from the kitchen... *She will not come to see me.* He stabs her with a long knife, stabs again and again; she lies on the floor — in blood! ... It's too quiet. There is no clink of silver, no water running on metal... Silence.... *But what is she doing?*

He clenches his fists and, his back against the wall, edges toward the door. Paper rustles faintly, a chair rocks, creaks. *Is she crying? She doesn't cry. Why should I?* Who can tell what she does?

She has cruel secrets, she frowns quietly, her moods shift like bats. *Why doesn't she smile?* She can be so nice—prettier than any one ... *than Susan?* He reaches into his pocket, past the letter, touching finally the cold piece of metal, taking it out. Heart-shaped locket of gold, reflecting the light overhead — a pale wavering moon. He draws in the chain his hand swallows the locket and closes. "Prettier than Susan," he whispers.

He thrusts the locket back. His eyes close slowly, then blink open. *Prettier than mother?* His hand moving back and forth along the chipped plaster of the wall. *You should love mother more — daddy too. I never see them. They have to work — they have to make money now.* Fingers digging into the wall: *They always stay away....* Again, he looks toward the door, trying to see through it. So kind sometimes: She gave him her music notebooks and helped him paste in pictures of composers, and now they were choosing ones for a new book on singers (he cried when she said they couldn't keep the one of the tall Black man dressed as a general or emperor because he didn't love his country — he'd tried to hide it, but she had found it). She keeps the books locked up in her bottom dresser drawer, it is their secret.... Dropping his hand, pushing the door open, crying: "I'm sorry, Elaine." He runs into the kitchen.

3.

She dabs her cheeks with pink tissue, her elbows on the table. She does not look up, and he approaches slower. "Elaine, I didn't mean anything ... I'm sorry." She turns to the wall, crushing the tissue in her hand. "Go away," she says. "But I didn't mean it. I — I thought you were dead." It is not even her —just a blouse, hands and arms, long black hair over shoulders. "Elaine! I didn't mean it!"

"You didn't mean it!" she screams. "I told you never to speak to me when I'm in the bathroom."

"But I thought you were dead. I didn't hear you."

"You're lying. I've always got to take care of you, and all you do is talk and talk: Elaine this, Elaine that." She turns to him, her eyes glaring, forcing him back. "I'm sixteen years old — sixteen. And I never have a moment to myself."

An ant scurries between his shoes, cut off from its clan, lost. "I have to take care of you all the time. Listen to you, cook for you, stay home with you — even on weekends. I haven't gone out in three weeks."

"We went to the movies."

"Danny and I took you with us."

"Elaine, I'm sorry. I'll tell you what: you can go out tonight — I'll stay by myself."

"And who'll take care of you?"

"I don't need anyone."

"You're afraid of the dark."

"I am not — I'll leave on the lights."

"And what happens when the kidnappers come?" His trembling fingers drum on his lips. "No — it's not your fault.... Besides, where would I go? Now—*now*! ...'

"You've already messed up tonight—and everything. It just isn't fair. You get everything you want: 'You're such a little boy!' But I—I don't even have a room to myself—or a mirror." She stops, her head lolls on her shoulder.

"What's wrong, Elaine?"

"Nothing—leave me alone."

"Can't I do anything? Tell me what's wrong."

She looks up, her eyes glinting. "I have to spend all my time with you and you won't leave me alone. Aren't I entitled to anything?"

"I'm sorry, Elaine. I'll be good. I won't bother you anymore."

"I can't even have any dates. I always have to take you or have boys over. And you're always in the way."

"I'm sorry."

"It isn't right for me to always have boys over."

"I'm—"

"If you say you're sorry once more, I'll kill you, you spoiled brat. I'll take a knife and cut off your head." He closes his eyes and covers his ears. "I'll cut off your head and then I won't have to see you or hear you anymore. And I'll have some peace and quiet."

4.

Before him, a plate of spaghetti. "Tuck your napkin in, I said. You'll get it all over you.... That's it." His fork trembles, catches the light overhead. "What's wrong? Can't you be still?" *Roll it on your fork, it slips off; get it to your mouth, it trails along your chin, leaves a smear of greasy red.* "Don't play with your food, eat it." His teeth chatter, he cannot stop them. He twirls the spaghetti round and round. "Come on, eat it." She shouldn't talk with her mouth full. The spaghetti drips on his chin, slides back onto the plate. He covers his mouth.

'Oh, you're such a baby." She leans over him, snatching his fork. "Look at yourself. You've got sauce all over your face… And now you're crying just because you've got sauce on your face."

"I am not crying. I won't ever cry again."

"I'll bet. Men don't cry, but you'll always cry, you're crying right now." He turns to the wall, she chops away at his spaghetti: *ka-plank, ka-plank.* "I don't know what's to become of you. Mel. You're so sensitive about everything.... Look, Mel. I've got sauce on me too." Slowly he turns. "You do not."

"Here, look close." Her lipstick-red lips—around them, a fringe of dull orange-red.

"Well?" Suddenly she sticks out her tongue, licks the tip of his nose. "Ha! Ha! Isn't that funny?... And look—on my blouse too." Tiny polkadots of orange-red on the white sticking out. "Yes, that's funny," he says, laughing with his sister. She cuts off her laugh, he jams his to a halt. She scowls.

"What's wrong, Elaine?" She scowls more, more. "Please—"

A great bubble rises from her stomach and ... explodes in her mouth. She laughs and laughs, rocking back and forth, stamping her feet, shaking her head from side to side. "Oh Mel, you're such a fraidy cat." Pointing her finger at him: "You're so funny. Ha! Ha!" Her glowing black hair swishes this way and that; he smiles, nodding shyly, laughing again. "Now come on," she orders. "Before it gets cold."

She returns to her chair and begins to eat; then he begins. She laughs again, spaghetti spurting out of her mouth onto the table. He yanks his mouthful down. "Look what you did, Elaine." She keeps chewing, bending from the waist, swaying, laughing with her mouth open.

And now he dares to ask his question: "Did you get my valentine?" Again his plate, the rhythmic eating.

"Yes. But you shouldn't have done it. You wasted your money."

He nibbles his food, says nothing. The spaghetti is paste, he plays with it. She keeps on: fork up, food in.

"Full already?" she asks at last, between bites.

"I'm not hungry." He smiles weakly and drops his fork.

"That's good. I made such a nice dessert and now I can eat it all by myself." She smacks her lips.

"What is it?"

"Oh, never mind. You're not hungry." She goes on eating, she hums a tune.

"Come on, Elaine."

"You really want to know?"

"Yes—come on, tell me what it is."

"No, you don't want dessert. You're too fat anyway."

"I'm hungry. Elaine! I'm hungry!"

"You're just saying that not to hurt my feelings because you know I spent a lot of time making that dessert."

"No I'm not."

"You don't care?"

"I didn't mean that—please!"

"Well I'm not sure ..."

"With sugar on it—come on!"

"All right, but if you don't like it, you better keep quiet."

She stretches, yawns, and, humming her tune, rises and walks slowly to the refrigerator, opening the door and standing in front of the shelves so he can't see. He bites his lip, waits. She glances over her shoulder. "Close your eyes—come on, close them."

Silver splotches erupt in the dark. Her skirt rustles.... She approaches—her lips stretched down, fangs instead of teeth; close-pinched, inflamed eyes—wild grey-streaked hair. Her bony long-nailed fingers hold a knife. The huge blade catches the kitchen light, blinds him. She plunges the knife—!

"Stop shaking your legs, Mel. Do you have to go to the bathroom?... Stop peeking. Don't you have any patience?" He covers his eyes again, but he has seen.

"Happy Valentine's Day to you —'

A cake—chocolate and pink, heart-shaped, with Mel in red jelly.

"Valentine's Day, dear Melvin—'

He throws his arms around her neck, jumping up and down. "Thought I'd forgotten you.... Come on, Mel, sit down."

"It looks so good."

The fork slips from his hand, he picks it up. "You really shouldn't have cake, you're getting so fat."

"But it's Valentine's Day, Elaine." She cranes her neck toward the clock, squinting.

"Yes, Valentine's Day."

5.

He swallows the M, the E and the L. She takes the dishes from the table, stacks them on the drainboard.

"Elaine? .... Can we listen to your records ... and ... work on the music notebooks? Can we?"

She lifts some plates out of the sink, onto the drainboard—
slam! "I can't. I have something to do."

"You never help me, Elaine. You always promise."

"And you always want things you shouldn't want."

She looks up at the clock, presses the plate edge against her chest and stares at him darkly.

"You never help me," he says weakly.

"I can't and that's that."

"It's not fair." She peers toward the hall, drums her fingers on the plate.

"I'm always alone," he says.

"Fair ... I'm the one who's not fair?"

"What, Elaine?"

"You didn't offer me any cake." He bites his lip. ... "You want some?"

"I had to remind you first."

"I'm sorry. Elaine. Here."

"No, I don't want it. If you're so stingy you won't give me one small piece."

"But here, Elaine."

"You just forgot that nice people share with each other. But you never felt like giving any cake to your sister."

"That's not so." *Why does she look at the clock?* ... Almost 7:30.

"Liar!" She jams the plate into the rack. "You're just a little liar who has to have his own way. Self self self. All the time." Once more he offers the cake. It rolls off—onto the table, bounding to the floor. "Look at the mess you've made. Look at it. I swear! I don't know what to do with you. All I give up—all the time. When I could be going out, I stay here with you. Cleaning your nose, wiping your behind." On his hands and knees, he fumbles after crumbs. "Get up from there, Mel. Of all the stupid things to do. Go away. Go and wash yourself"

6.

The door locked, he washes his face of the heatsting, the redness; then sits, doubled over, elbows grooving his thighs, his hands cupped under his chin. The room is narrow and damp. His breathing fills it, reaches every corner, rings the iron pipes. His sounds echo, return evenly, the same—yet somehow magnified: freer, more final, complete. He is the room. Nothing can harm him. The mirror on the wall reflects the wall. But suddenly, the scraping of plates, the distant clash of silver. *If I breathe louder...* But he cannot help swallowing air and leaning forward: the scuffle of shoes, the rising dirge of water turned on ... then, a sharp ring—close by, off to the side; again—from *their room.* The water dies; footsteps tap nearer, pass by — hitting faster, then stopping. A half-ring. "Hello, Danny..."A door squeaks, clicks.

He reaches past the card, drawing out the locket. Not looking, he traces his finger around the edge, stopping at the chainloop, starting again. Helplessly, he tries to hear, catching: "Danny ... Danny.... but Danny—" She slams the receiver, the door hits the wall. She runs past him again, through the livingroom. *She's going to her room.*

Now his room shrinks, while he grows bigger—monstrous. His limbs press all four walls. He is cramped and squeezed, the ceiling bows his head. He cannot move or breathe, and yet—he grows.

On the ceiling, paint has peeled in all directions, plaster bare in the center.

"Mel!" He sits up as she draws closer, closer to the door. "Mel!" The knob turns. "Mel, open up. I've got to speak to you."

"What do you want?"

"I've got to speak to you — please!" He goes to the door, stands before it: he clenches his hand around the locket, puts it behind his back. "Mel!" He hesitates and… opens the door.

"In my bottom dresser drawer, Mel.... You know, the locket Danny gave me ... you know the one ... I've got to have it."

He steps back. "I don't have it."

"But it's not there. You're the only one who knew where it was—in the drawer under the notebooks ... I told you yesterday I had to give it back ... and it's not there!"

"I don't have your locket." His face wells with heat, again he steps back.

"Mel, I've got to have that locket. I won't punish you, I promise. If you know where it is, please give it to me ... please." She starts to cry. "I won't hurt you, Mel. But I've got to have it." Crying, her legs tottering.

"You won't hurt me?"

Her eyes meet him. "Mel—no! ... You have it?"

He shuts his eyes and holds out his hand. "In your hand!?" He opens his fist, palm up, not seeing her at all: the small locket — old, tarnished, reflecting the bathroom light: the pale, misshapen moon. "Thank you, Mel."

"The chain's broken."

"Broken?"

"I broke it."

"That's all right, Mel. I can tell Danny—" She stops. The floor, a checkerboard of tiles — black and white. "Mel, did you mean to give this to someone?"

"I gave it."

"Gave it!... But—"

He springs for the door. She grabs him by the shoulders. "Let me go! Let me go!" He tries to wrench free.

"Not till you tell me who you—"

"I won't!" He lunges again. "Tell me."

"I gave it to Susan for her birthday last week. I had to give her something ... I thought you wouldn't care. I gave it to her."

"But it was my locket."

"I know, I know!"

"Well...?"

"Well, yesterday you said you had to give it back, and today I asked Susan for it, and she said, ask Mary Alt — and I saw Mary Alt wearing it. I said where'd you get that, and she said Susan gave it to her. I said, give it to me. But she wouldn't.... So I ripped it off her neck. And she started crying. And — and Miss McCarthy sent me to the principal and I sat in her office all afternoon. And I missed the party."

"Mel!"

"I didn't think you'd care."

"Poor Mel." Everything blurs. Her warm hands caress his neck. "Poor Mel."

"Hit me if you want." He falls against her.

"That's right, Mel. You cry." He tries to break away. "I'm sorry, Mel. Don't worry. I'll leave you ... by yourself. When you're ready, you come in and help me. There's a mob of dishes to do." She kisses his forehead. "Just take your time."

7.

He does not walk at all, it is the floor that moves—moves not only across, but slowly, slowly up, lifting him into the kitchen—without his doing anything but stare at the floor, not yet awake, not knowing. But he has not collided with chairs or walk, and he is in the kitchen.

'Don't stand there like a corpse. Get a towel." He takes one down, doubling it over his arm, then lifting it and pinching along the fold. "Hurry. I've nowhere to put the dishes." A large stack already—from yesterday, this morning, tonight: different-colored plates and pots and glasses in the draining rack, reflecting the dull light. "Don't look so downhearted.... There aren't that many."

Carefully, without upsetting the others, he removes a plate and begins wiping—slowly. Finishing, he places it on the table, takes up another, wipes it... wearily. He closes his eyes, and all the dishes—the whole ugly terrible heap: solid, cold—fly off the edge of the spinning globe. Calendar pages flip over and dishes sit in piles to be cleaned and hidden behind cabinet doors — dumbly, wearily ... again, again: endlessly. *Work ... yes! Work is what's so bad....* Again the dishes, the silverware fly away. Everything disappears from the face of the earth.

"Come on ... I put your cake in the icebox. You can have it later." He smiles weakly, affects a big, manly voice — drying a glass:

"So many dishes, Elaine. So many dishes."

She throws a towel over her head, grabs the broom and leans on it — puckering her lips and speaking in a high, squeaking voice: "So many dishes to wash. I don't know when I'll rest. So many dishes."

"Oh, I don't look like that."

"That's you."

"No, it isn't."

"So many dishes to wash."

"You've got a towel on your head. You're not supposed to."

"You've got me there." She takes off the towel, casts the broom aside.

"Really, Elaine, it doesn't seem like we'll ever stop doing dishes."

"That's right. It shall go on forever and ever. Your whole life shall be spent drying dishes ... if you don't start drying."

She turns on the water, sprays the pots and pans. Reluctantly, he takes up a plate, working now fast, now slow. He starts, stops, stares, starts again. He dries and redries the same dish.

"Mel..." She stares out the window, her back to him. "Danny's coming over.... That's why I need to give him back the ... the locket. He's taking someone else to the dance tonight... at school. And I said it's all over.... That's why I had to have the locket... to give it back," she says, turning to him- her face so pretty, so plump.... *Her eyes are so sad.* He raises his hand and gropes clumsily along her cheek. "It's all right Mel. It's not so bad, not so bad at all. And look: When Danny comes, I want you to say hello

and shake his hand. And then I want you to say good night and go
to your room. Understand?"

"Yes."

"Then let's finish these dishes." She takes her towel and helps
him dry. He barely moves "Mel, smile."

"I hate it here, Elaine."

"We won't be here always."

"Someday you'll be married, won't you?"

"I guess so, 'Mel… Maybe …I hope so."

"And you'll go far away and live in the country. I won't see
you."

"You'll see me. Besides, that's a long time from now. You'll
be a man then. It won't matter so much."

Outside the snow is still falling—white spots against tall
shadowy buildings. He cranes his neck to see beyond them.
"Elaine?... Not tonight, but some time ... when you get a chance—
you know... Well, could you help me work on the notebook—of
singers.... Just to get me started...."

"I'll help you tomorrow night. I promise."

"You always promise."

"Well, this time I mean it. Tomorrow night I'll help you."

"Swear to God and cross your heart, no—"

"No crossed fingers.... Now smile.... That's a little better."

"If you can't make it tomorrow, Sunday's fine."

"Tomorrow night... I promise."

She looks him up and down and exclaims, "Mel!"; she turns
away, then back suddenly. "Mel ... I know what: Let's build a city."

"What do you mean?"

"Let's build New York—with dishes, silly." He creases his
chin. "Here." She goes to the table and puts a glass in a saucer, dries
a fork and sticks it in the glass, asking, "What's that?"

"Give me a hint."

"The saucers are an island."

"The—the Statue of Liberty!"

They laugh. "You see? We can build a whole city while we dry the dishes. We'll try and guess what we build."

Quickly, he dries two cups, turns them upside down on the table, and lays a fork across. "What's that?"

"I don't know."

"Oh yes you do. Come on."

"I know!"

"Sure you do!"

"It's a telephone!"

"No!"

"Why, sure it is. Here, look at the—"

"Elaine, it's not a telephone. It's the George Washington Bridge."

"Oh ... oh!"

"You knew what it was."

"No I didn't. I thought—"

"Come on, Elaine. Don't lie. Come on. You knew it was the George Washington Bridge."

"No, I swear..."

"Come on, Elaine." He laughs suddenly. "You knew and you just said that. You just tried to fool me, didn't you? Didn't you?"

They both bend with laughter. They laugh and laugh. Then she hands him a pot. She curtseys, he bows—and they set to work building their city, while the snow falls and the light seems to make the dishes glitter and dazzle.

The Landlord

1.

At first Mr. Hirsh would come home from work carrying his paper, and if you were bending over, he'd swat you and say "hi, boy," and you'd look up and see a red face laughing and sad fuzzy eyes suddenly lit up.

We wondered why the lit-up eyes seemed so sad, but we didn't say it out loud. We only knew that Mr. Hirsh was wonderful—to be always laughing when his eyes were so sad: that was something.

We didn't have much time for old people. We came home from school, had our milk and cookies, and then stood outside thumping the ball against the stoop, letting it bounce up and trying to catch it before it bounced again.

But Mr. Hirsh came into the game, and he didn't have to win all the time. He'd say, "I'm Joe DiMaggio who are you?" Bobby was Dixie Walker, and I was stuck with Sid Gordon. But it was all right. Sometimes Sid Gordon could win.

And Mr. Hirsh knew not to play too much. Instead, he trimmed the bushes along the walk, so the ball wouldn't get stuck. And when we'd lose one, he'd get another.

"With all these bushes, you're bound to lose a few," he'd say, "and it's my fault." But we knew it wasn't. Sometimes the ball would end in the sewer, but he'd pretend it was lost in the bushes and still get us another one-fast too. He said he'd come home from work and hunted them while we were at school. But we knew that wasn't so.

Of course, we never told him we knew, we were so happy to keep on playing. And after a while we'd say the ball was lost in the bushes, even when they went down the sewer. We'd say that without his saying it first. And we knew we were lying, and I even think he knew we knew. But he took it to mean we were friends I guess, and still got us new balls just as we thought he would. Then we really started lying, saying we'd lost balls when we hadn't. And what could Mr. Hirsh do? He was stuck with his story about the bushes. We got a lot of balls that way.

That was in the fall. My parents had just moved into the neighborhood. They worked long hours and weren't around much. Mr. and Mrs. Hirsh were the landlords. Bobby lived next door. He had lots of friends, but he played ball with me.

In the winter it wasn't stoopball because of the snow but it was Christmas and sledding. Mr. Hirsh bought me and Bobby a sled, and he'd go over to the park with us and watch us sometimes and join in too. Only there wasn't any way we could play games with him now or make the most of him. He didn't seem so old now. He almost seemed like one of us. We liked it better in the fall.

One day Bobby said, "Mr. Hirsh's got gray hair and wrinkles." That was a silly thing to say. Any fool could see it. But I saw Bobby had a special reason to talk. "My mother says his face is red 'cause he's got a bad heart and the blood's all going to his head. She says he'll die before long."

"Yeah?" I say.

"Well, my mother said Mrs. Hirsh's pregnant," he says.

"What's that?"

"She's pregnant—that's what she said. And she said he's pretty old."

I couldn't get what Bobby meant. But soon I saw that Mrs. Hirsh was getting really fat in a funny way, and she and Mr. Hirsh looked happy. I could hear them laughing a lot upstairs. And they were always going out now, like never before, and having lots of people over, and there was so much laughing and yelling I couldn't sleep sometimes at night. And Mr. Hirsh didn't have that sad look anymore. I knew what that was, I'd seen it all before.

I said to Bobby, "Mrs. Hirsh isn't pregnant, she's gonna have a baby."

And Bobby said, "That's what pregnant is."

But I knew I was right and he was wrong. He was just trying to slide into being right. That's the way Bobby was. With him I was always Sid Gordon.

So I began to look at Mr. Hirsh in a special way now. We didn't like this baby because we knew what it would do to us. We were waiting for the spring because we wanted a big stash of pink balls. Bobby said we could have a raffle like at church and make money. But we had only ten balls between us, and you couldn't make much that way. We knew what happened when people had babies.

So we had to look at Mr. Hirsh in a different way now. Not that he changed much, but he did change some, you could see it. He still said hi and swatted us and went to the park and brought us candy sometimes. But more often he'd stay home because his wife was sick, he'd say. And even when he'd go, he'd get a dreamy look and say something he'd said before — like "It's so cold your nose could break off," something silly like that. And he'd sound hollow, like the sound came through a straw stuck in his throat. You could tell he wasn't in the park but somewhere else — in Mrs. Hirsh's stomach, I guessed. He just wasn't with us.

"My mother says he's rehearsing," Bobby said.

"What's that?"

That Bobby always came up with words you couldn't understand — just so if he was wrong, he could say he was right later. "Like in a play. She says he's rehearsing at being a father."

Well, that explained it. And all along we thought we'd had him charmed — the way you can do it with old people that are lonely and sad with troubles, and wish they were kids again. You can really take those kind. But here he'd been taking *us*. We were his baby till that baby came—and soon there wouldn't be any pink balls or anything.

Sure enough, some weeks went by and Mr. Hirsh stopped going to the park. He'd still be friendly, but he didn't care much about us. We could see it. We were mad, only what could we do? We talked it out one day walking home from school.

"We gotta do something," I said.

"We sure do," Bobby said. But I could tell he just said that, he didn't care much. He'd only make some plans you could never use, and then when one ofhis didn't work, he'd say I told you so. Nothing mattered that much to him. He could always go back to his friends or go home and have a good time. But he and Mr. Hirsh were the only ones I talked to.

So Bobby just did as usual, saying what I'd said, waiting for me to make a plan so he could say how silly it was and then make some crazy one you could never do. But that wasn't because it wasn't a good plan — oh no! It was the plan, only he'd have to work it with a Sid Gordon. That's the way he was.

I had to think of something, but I couldn't. So, I started talking, thinking maybe I'd get so worked up, I'd dream up something so good, Bobby'd have to go along.

"You know what he's done. Now he's gonna have a kid and I bet he won't even let us play on that stoop. He won't even let us breathe too loud."

"But what can we do?" said Bobby. He wanted to look like he meant business, to make me make a fool of myself. But this time I fooled *him* — because I was worked up and I'd already hit on a plan.

"We'll just not go with him to the park. And if he comes anyway or finds us out, we won't pay any attention to him. We'll act like he's not there."

"That's no good," Bobby said, like always. "He's still fun sometimes, so why spoil things ahead of time?"

"Because if he can't rehearse now, he won't be a good father. And then he won't have fun unless we're around."

"It's no good." And now I knew Bobby was saying no for sure this time. "He's stopped rehearsing," he said.

I was so mad I could scream. And I just looked at him — with his red hair and pushed-up nose. He was Dixie Walker all right. And what got me mad was he just wanted to look smart. He wasn't thinking about that raffle either. He just didn't care that much. He just stood there trying to think up a crazy plan we couldn't do, so we'd end up doing nothing. And I knew I had to think up another too. I knew I had to out-Bobby Bobby. And the funny thing is, I did it — and fast too, before he said a thing.

"Ok, Mr. Dixie Walker bigshot," I said, "I've got one you can't say no to."

Well that stopped him. I never came back with another one before, and he wasn't too happy about it. All he could say is, "Yeah? What is it?"

"Stop the baby."

"What?"

"He wants a baby, right? So, stop the baby!" You could see he'd never heard anything so wild and didn't even believe I could think it up. So now he said, "Ok Sid Gordon, you tell me. How do you stop the baby?"

And then I said it all, my eyes flashing into the trees and along the snow piles — like I'd discovered gold. I said it all and changed everything — felt things I'd never felt before, and changed everything inside me, fast.

"Easy," I said. "Mrs. Hirsh's got it. In her belly, right? ... And Mr. Hirsh is never home all day, is he? ... So one day when he's at work, we go up to Mrs. Hirsh and say, Mrs. Hirsh, someone's calling you downstairs. You better go see. And soon as she starts down, we come up behind her and give her a push, and down she goes — woosh! And then — and then —."

I was stuck, I couldn't finish. But not Bobby. He was jumping up and down, pushing off on my shoulder. "No more baby!" he shouts. Something hurt in my stomach. I didn't know what it was or why — not yet. But it started when I was talking, and now I just watched Bobby and hurt more. "Stop the baby!" he was yelling.

"We get a rope and tie it across the stairs, so when we push, she'll go down for sure! We got a rope too — on the sled!"

"It's no good," I said, and I stopped in the street.

"But you just said —"

"I changed my mind. I know it won't work now. You can't stop babies."

"But I saw it on TV. This man kills his kid—woosh! down the stairs!"

"I won't do it. I can't." And all at once I was crying — like a fool. I turned my head so he wouldn't see.

"I don't get it," Bobby said. "You think up a good way to get at old Hirsh."

And now I was getting mad and I knew I couldn't hold it back for long. "I don't want to think," I said. "I don't want a plan."

"Come on, Mel. It's a neat idea —"

"I don't want your ideas. I had enough of them."

"Mine!"

"Just like yours."

"Well, jeez, you don't have to — say!"

He tried to spin me around. "Leave me alone!" I shouted.

"I get it," he said, getting sharp all at once. "You don't want to hurt old Hirsh."

"No," I said. "I don't." "You don't want to woosh! — down the stairs!"

"Stop it Bobby."

He kept flying at me — "Woosh! Woosh!"

"Stop it!"

"You don't like it."

"That's right," I said. "I don't like it and I don't like you because you made me think it and you like it. I don't like your plans — or TV shows or raffles. And they don't mean a thing anyway."

And now Bobby was mad because he thought I wasn't fair. And he was right in a way, I guess, but in another way he wasn't.

"You like Mr. Hirsch," he said. And he started dancing and chanting around me. "You like Mr. Hirsh!"

"Better than you any day."

Bobby stopped. "Ok. You like him. When that baby comes, he won't even look at you."

"That's not true. I won't let that happen!"

"No! *I* won't. Me! 'Cause I'll… stop the baby!" "No!"

"Woosh!" he shouted, dancing again. "If you won't, I will! I'll stop it! Woosh!" And then he hit me hard in the belly, and then he ran and said, "You wait." And I just sat down against a bank of snow all hurt and scared inside.

2.

So now everything was turned around. And I thought what a big fool I was, but there was nothing I could do about it now. I just thought, Bobby is gone and Mr. Hirsh is on his way. And I thought ok, if that's how it has to be, ok. I'll go after Mr. Hirsh and try not to lose him. I'll be such a friend of his, he won't forget me for anything.

And I had a way to be his friend, because what if Bobby really tried to stop the baby? And I felt good for a minute thinking I really had a job to do. And then I had that hurt feeling in my stomach again, and felt bad for all kinds of things, like for taking the pink balls. Then I got scared, because I could almost see what Bobby was planning. And I thought how stupid it all was and how Mr. Hirsh wouldn't be my friend no matter what, so I couldn't warn him because he might not believe me and ask questions and get mad— or something like that. But I said, if Bobby's going to stop the baby, you've got to stop him. And I felt better and decided to get to work and stop thinking, which was smart, because that's what started my trouble anyhow.

But I found out there wasn't too much I could do. The first few days I'd meet Mr. Hirsh coming home, but we just couldn't seem to talk to each other. He'd still bring presents, but not for me.

And he didn't try to swat me or say let's go to the park. He didn't even ask why Bobby didn't play with me anymore — why Bobby was back with his old gang, and I was by myself. It was bad. Every day I'd just say some words that didn't mean a thing and then I'd try to hint at the real thing. But I couldn't get it out, especially when you could tell he just wanted to go upstairs. So after a while, I didn't try hard to see him anymore. He looked all nervous and worried anyway, and I decided I'd do better right now just keeping my eyes open.

But the less I saw Mr. Hirsh, the more worried I got, watching for Bobby, afraid he'd make his move. He didn't do a thing, but that just made me see he was trying to get my guard down. He even tried to talk to me once, but I wouldn't give him the chance to fool me. And after that, whenever I'd see him, he'd go woosh! and laugh at me. That's all he'd say—and those friends of his said it too: "Woosh!" they'd shout at me. The worst of it was, I'd see him all the time because I had to make sure he didn't try something and seeing him made me remember all the good times we'd had. That didn't make me want to talk to him really. But I was getting lonely—more and more. I had no one to say a thing to, except my parents when they came home from work late at night. And they didn't say much. Some days, except for school, all I heard was *woosh!* I'd come home and have cookies and then turn on my dad's victrola. And all the time I'd be looking out the window, waiting for Bobby. And then Mr. Hirsh'd come home and wave hi and go upstairs, and I knew Mrs. Hirsh was safe another day. I wouldn't have to worry after that, but somehow it didn't help much. I felt empty in my stomach then. And it wasn't that I didn't like victrola music. I got to like it better all the time.

Day after day I just sat there listening and watching and every day, I got more lonely and scared. And I wanted time to stop, but I knew it wouldn't. And I knew I should tell Mr. Hirsh, but then I'd think maybe it's not going to happen. Then I'd turn up a symphony loud to drown me out, and I'd try to see how Bobby'd do it. I'd drift away in the music and see someone wearing a mask tiptoe up the back stairs. You couldn't see his face, but it had to be Bobby. And each day he'd get a step higher and closer to Mrs. Hirsh. And she'd scream Mel! because I was the only one home, I guess. And I'd run up and stop him just in time. And Mr. Hirsh would thank me and give me something good. And after that I'd feel good and then I felt empty again. So soon I kept it a secret and didn't let them know how I'd saved them. But it was getting harder all the time. Each day Bobby got higher and closer and I just did stop him. And now he carried a gun and now a knife. And the gun and the knife got bigger, and we were running out of steps.

Then in the schoolyard Bobby yelled, "Hey Mel! My mother says it's any day now." And, like a plan, I looked around and saw Penny Carter skipping rope and the rope went *woosh, woosh*! And I knew what it all meant. Mrs. Hirsh was having her baby soon and Bobby was going to get her first. Not with a gun or a knife. But with a rope just the way he said.

It was a race. All the way home, I saw Bobby in his mask climbing the stairs and me chasing after, and Mrs. Hirsh tripped over Penny Carter's rope and screamed. And then the scream was the baby's, and, Mr. Hirsh stood there holding the baby and smiling. And I don't know which made me feel worse. But I knew I couldn't stand it anymore. I knew it was my last chance with Mr. Hirsh. I'd have to tell him now, even though I didn't want to and was scared of him and what he'd say. In some way I didn't want the waiting to end. I wanted it to go on forever if it only didn't hurt so much. I always knew I'd have to tell him and take my chances, and that really scared me and gave me that empty feeling more than anything.

After Mr. Hirsh came home, I heard him shoveling coal in the cellar furnace. I knew this was it. I took a deep breath and went downstairs. Sure enough, he was there. But when I saw him, I froze. He was leaning over his shovel and staring into the fire. His face was bright red from embers, and his eyes were bright too. His teeth showed all white, and I thought, if he laughs it's the end of the world. I just had to stay still and wait for him to get back to work and look like Mr. Hirsh. But he just stood there a long time and didn't move. I had to say something, or we'd be there always.

"Mr. Hirsh," I said. But I must have whispered it because he still didn't move. Now I thought it wasn't him, so I shrieked, "Mr. Hirsh!" And this time he heard me and it was him.

He moved out of the light and said hi.

"Hi," I said. "Can I give you a hand?"

"That's ok, Mel, just one more to go."

It was like I wasn't there. He went over to the bin and lifted a shovelful of coal. And I looked all around trying to find I don't know what. There were piles of soggy newspaper and rags all over. The outside was blocked by snow on the windows. Even with the heat it was cold and damp. There wasn't a thing I could do, and I wanted to go away. But I couldn't get my feet to take me—not now.

Mr. Hirsh poured coal on the fire and shut the door, then he walked over to his worktable. On it was an upside-down basket with rocking horse legs standing in the air. While he looked at it, I came down off the stairs and moved close up to him.

"It's for the baby," he said, rubbing his hand along the side. "I'm sanding it down."

"Can I help?"

"No thanks. Not enough work for two." He started folding a piece of sandpaper.

"Mr. Hirsh, I hardly see you anymore."

"Oh I see you." But he was turned away from me, didn't even look up.

"No, you always go right up to Mrs. Hirsh. You didn't even tell me about the baby."

He squinted at me hard, his eyes hard. "Your folks told you… " He didn't wait for an answer, he started scraping the wood. "I guess I should've done it," he said in a quiet voice. And then he got louder. "But you found out anyway… everyone did… They couldn't believe it—I couldn't... at first." He wasn't talking to me. He was soft and loud and now he was soft again and a little sad. "But it's true — any day now"

"Mr. Hirsh!"

He looked up, his lips were tight, and his face was bright red from the light by the table. And now he looked down at the basket again, as if I hadn't said a thing. "It's my old cradle," he said. "Fifty-four years old... I got him lots of new things... You'd think maybe—"

"It'll be fine, Mr. Hirsh." He was quiet for a minute, we just stood there.

"What color you gonna paint her?"

"Blue," he said. And now he sanded one of the rockers — a long time. I looked around the table and shelves at the jars of nails and screws — and then at a stack of dusty old magazines. I picked one up and looked through it. It looked all right, but then I couldn't read anymore, so I put it down. And then on the shelf I saw a bucket.

"This the paint?"

"Uh huh-" he said, not looking up.

"Can I see?" I jumped up to get it, and on the way down, I bumped against the cradle. It would have crashed, but Mr. Hirsh stopped it. He grabbed the bucket from me and pried the lid.

"You see now?" he said, sticking it in my nose.

Then he closed it and put it back — all before I could see it — and started sanding again.

"Could I help you when you start painting?"

And this time he breathed deep and looked me in the eye. "It's a small cradle — for a baby, see? It only takes minutes to paint — and I want to do it."

"Sorry," I said. I mean I heard it come out. And then I was so mad at saying it, I said, "You don't want me around, do you?"

"Now, Mel—"

"You used to play with me and Bobby. But now—"

"Mel, it's just that Mrs. Hirsh needs me now — and there's so much to do."

But I knew he was just saying that, and besides, I had to start telling him.

"You don't even know about Bobby. You don't even know we're not friends anymore."

"You and Bobby—?"

"You didn't even know." "I been so busy, Mel, I—" "You don't even know us anymore. When that baby comes—" "When my kid's here, we'll all be friends."

Well that stopped me and I couldn't say it. Because I knew then that the reason I was going to was so he'd say what he just said — and I knew that wasn't right. So I looked at him hard and said, "How can you be friends with a baby, Mr. Hirsh?"

"Not friends, but... " He couldn't finish it. I just turned away and picked up the magazine. After a while he said, "You and Bobby had a fight, huh? Well, kids always fight, you'll get over it."

And that got me mad, so I tried again. "Bobby's gonna stop—"

"I know, Mel, I know."

But he didn't. He just didn't care. And all at once I missed Bobby and it didn't seem right to tell on him — not for Mr. Hirsh. If he didn't care, why should I?

"Anyway," he said, "You've got other kids to play with."

"I don't have any kids!" I screamed. "They're all Bobby's friends anyway. They all stick with him. I don't have anyone!" And I said this to give him a last chance — to see what he would say. And I knew all over again I had to tell; no matter what he thought of me or Bobby or what I thought of him, or why I told, he had to know. But just then, Mr. Hirsh changed the subject.

"Look, Mel." He picked up the stack of magazines. "How'd you like to have them? They're full of pictures and stories — see? Like the one you're looking at. Lots of things about pirates and ships . . ." He kept turning pages and showing me all this stuff. And

I did like pirates and pictures, but I couldn't look at them. Besides, Mr. Hirsh was blocking the light, but he would never think of that. "Like to have "em?" he said.

I felt so tired, all the blood was draining out of me. Those weeks of watching were too much trouble, and all Mr. Hirsh's words were just too much to stand. And I saw all at once that Mr. Hirsh was scared. He was scared of the baby, so he didn't want me around, even though he might want to, because it made him feel bad. He stood there showing me these magazines, and all the time I felt how tired I was of his presents and how I hated being given things and how bad it made me feel. And then I looked at Mr. Hirsh and at the cradle and paint bucket. And I knew I'd made it all up. That Mrs. Hirsh would have the baby and Bobby wouldn't even try to stop it. And I'd been afraid of Mr. Hirsh finding out, when all the time it didn't matter and I'd just been playing a stupid game with myself.

"Well, how about it?"

"No thanks, Mr. Hirsh," I said, trying to smile.

"You're sure?" And he held them out like he was just dying for me to take them. "I've got too much schoolwork to read magazines," I said. "I better go up and do it too."

And sure enough, he didn't die or carry on. He wasn't even sorry to hear me go. "Ok, Mel, you do your work if you have to." And I walked off and left him by the table. "Mel!" he called when I reached the stairs. "If you want, you can help me paint this sometime." But I knew enough to know he didn't mean it, and I'd decided I didn't want to be where I wasn't wanted.

I didn't do homework; I sat by the window and waited for Bobby to come from playing with his gang. I felt good when I saw him down the street. I ran out to tell him how wrong I'd been. "Bobby," I said, "You're not gonna stop the baby."

"Of course not," he said. "And I'm not gonna talk to you."

"But how come—?"

"Because you thought up that plan and my mother says I shouldn't."

"But I'm not gonna do it." And I could see he was getting madder every minute.

"You planned it. You planned it and said it was my plan."

"You'd think it up, Bobby. You liked it."

"My mother said I wouldn't do that!" he yelled. "She said I should tell Mr. Hirsh."

"No, Bobby."

"And that's what I'm gonna do."

"No!"

"I'm gonna tell him right now." He walked off past his house and I watched him go up our driveway and through the back door.

I just stood there and walked in circles and watched it get dark. And then I went in and sat in the dark thinking what I could do. And all these bad thoughts went through my head, so I had to turn on the victrola to drown them out. I turned it on loud and tried to drift away. And all at once there was a knock on the ceiling that made me jump up all scared, as if someone was in my head. I knew it was Mr. Hirsh knocking to make me quiet, so I turned off the music, but that made me feel worse. And I didn't want to see him, but now I did all over again—and I couldn't. I kept saying to myself ok, ok. And after a while, when I was sure no one was listening, I tip-toed out the back door downstairs to the cellar. The magazines were still next to the cradle on the table. I grabbed up a bunch and locked the door behind me.

3.

I had to have something. I read the stories about pirates and ships. I brought the victrola to my room and listened to symphonies in the dark and told myself the stories over and over 'til I fell asleep. And then I cut out the pictures and nailed them on the walls, even when I knew I shouldn't. They were all pretty girls and cruel pirates and had names like Lady Jane and Princess Ann and Bad Sam. A few times, when the music got loud, Mr. Hirsh knocked and I turned it down. I'd look at the pictures and not feel so bad. The girls were still pretty, even Bad Sam was all right, and I could still hear the music. So, I got to like my room more and more. It was mine. I wouldn't let anyone see it.

Then one night I heard the Hirshes come down the back stairs. I heard Mrs. Hirsh moaning and Mr. Hirsh saying doctor, somebody. I was perfectly still. I didn't move or breathe till they were down. Doors opened and slammed, the car started and backed down the driveway.

"It's ok," I whispered. "They're not coming back. It's not real. They're not."

Then I turned on the light and looked at my pictures. Lady Jane smiled and I knew she was more real than Mr. or Mrs. Hirsh.

"And Bobby isn't real," I whispered, and felt strange somehow. I looked out my window and there was Bobby's house. But I worked it out — it was only there when I saw it, and when I didn't see it, it wasn't there. I pulled down the shade.

That was the night I made up my own stories. I was Captain Lopez. I saved all the girls and gave pirate treasure to the poor. The next day I found a long stick and taped a piece of wood across it. And each night I made up stories and practiced sword fights with the music going and the pretty girls flashing past me.

But then came the last night when I was in bed half-asleep, I heard a noise. I couldn't tell what. And then I heard it again and knew the baby was there and was crying. I tried not to hear, I covered my ears with the pillow. But I couldn't stop it, it was too loud. I turned on the light and put on the victrola, but I still could hear the baby crying. I tried to think up stories, I got up and walked around and still it was there. I got my sword and started fighting. I saw the girls on the walls and heard the baby and turned the music louder. I was Captain Lopez, Bad Sam kidnapped Lady Jane. I caught up to the pirates and swung over on a rope. I killed one and two and three — and they were all dead. There was only Bad Sam and Lady Jane, she cried for me to save her. I chased Bad Sam around the ship, around chairs over the bed. He almost got me, but I flew past him, into the closet and out. Over we went, back and forth across the bed He tripped and fell, Lady Jane smiled and cried Mel! Mel! and I leaped on Bad Sam and stabbed him through—crash! The bed fell down.

Mr. Hirsh called "Mel!" He'd come into our house, stamped through the rooms and sprung open my door. "There's a baby upstairs!"

He stared at me over the bed posts, his face angry and red, and then he looked surprised. I was in my underwear twisted in the blankets on the mattress on the floor with the sword in my hand. I watched him see the chair and the clothes from the closet on the floor, and then my girls and pirates on my walls. Then his eyes came back at me.

"Didn't you hear me knock? What the hell have you been up to?"

"I stole the pictures," I said.

"What?" He made a face and turned off the music.

"I stole the magazines and tore the pictures out."

"But I said you could have them."

"I stole them. Like I stole the pink balls."

"Pink balls! My kid can't sleep!"

"You know. You know I want to kill him."

"Kill him! Are you crazy?"

"Bobby told you."

"I haven't seen Bobby in weeks."

And then I knew he didn't know. Bobby hadn't told him. He'd played a trick because he hated me. But I couldn't stop, it didn't matter. I laughed and laughed.

"What's with you, Mel? You stop it and tell me."

"I wanted to stop him, tie a rope across the stairs and trip Mrs. Hirsh and — woosh!" I swished the sword over and over. "Woosh!"

"Stop it Mel!" He grabbed the sword and pulled me up so I was screaming in his red face. "I took the balls. I lied to you and got them. I stole the pictures and nailed them up 'cause I knew you'd hate it!"

He shook me back and forth, the room went crazy. "Stop it! Stop it!" he shouted.

"I will! I'll trip him! Woosh!" He squeezed and stopped me and threw me hard on the bed. "Now you—calm down!"

I wanted to cry but I didn't. I bit my lip and stared at him. He stared back and then he looked around the room, turning the sword in his hand and talking almost to himself. "I don't believe it. If I thought you meant all this—" He looked at me again.

"No! It's crazy. You're alone too much is all. Your folks—"

And then I knew I wanted only one thing from him in the world. "Say I'm no good," I said. "Say I'm bad."

"Look Mel." And he talked slow and mean. "I know I should maybe see you more. But I got a baby now and you're going to have to be quiet. A baby needs quiet."

"Hit me!" I yelled. "Say I'm bad."

"It's not for me to do!"

"The cradle's old. You're too old."

"All right," he said, and his face got tighter and redder than ever. "All right." His hands shook and he saw he was holding the sword, and swung it in the air, with the sword going whoosh! whoosh! "I'm old and you're bad!"

I felt faint and dizzy, as though I was light floating round and round. And I could see how glad he was to say what he said and not to have to worry about me anymore. And I was even sorry for him, because I knew he knew what it meant . . . But then he did something I didn't count on. He did it and made everything terrible forever.

"I'm gonna tear down these pictures," he whispered. And he went along the walls ripping them off and tearing them.

"No, Mr. Hirsh — please!" I grabbed onto his legs and tried to stop them. "Don't do it."

He dragged me along on my knees till I couldn't hold on. I sprawled on the floor and watched him tear them down till there weren't any left. "There," he said. "And don't you put up any new ones."

I wanted to say something, to tell him he didn't have to do that. But I couldn't say a thing. I looked at his face—flushed full of pain and anger—and I heard his words smash in my head.

"I'll be watching, so don't you put up any pictures or run around the room or play that damned music. I got a baby to take care of. So don't you make her cry again —or do anything, or I'll make you wish you hadn't. You hear? You be quiet or I'll fix you good."

He turned his back and left the room. I stayed put 'til I heard him on the stairs and then I got up and shut my door. I threw the pictures and pieces of wood in the basket and yanked out the nails. I picked up the chair and clothes, I worked the mattress till I got it back up. Then I straightened the blankets and got in bed. I could see holes in the walls from the nails. And upstairs I could hear the baby screaming and the Hirshes talking. And I knew even then they'd always be there. And Mr. Hirsh would always watch me, he'd watch me and warn me and never let me forget. And if I put up pictures, he'd tear them down. And if I played music loud, he'd knock on the ceiling and I'd remember. And I tried to think of something new, someone, but I was scared to. And I knew if he'd hit me, it would have been better. But now I couldn't stop 'til I made him hit me — and I knew he never would. I leaned out of bed and pulled over the basket and found Lady Jane. She was all crumpled up and torn— only half there, one eye gone. And I kissed her goodbye and I cried.

I lay still in bed and cried inside me. And I thought of the pirates inside and my room, and about when I was Sid Gordon. And then I saw Bobby. He had a mask. He climbed, he tied the rope across the stairs. Mrs. Hirsh screamed, Mel! And then I knew I was everyone—the Hirshes screaming for help, Bobby slashing with his knife—and even Mr. Hirsh's baby dying in Mrs. Hirsh's stomach. And all the time I was the boy who lived downstairs.

Book Two. Pre-Teen Times

The Restaurant

Elizabeth was known as a center for Singer Sewing Machines and other companies. But, throughout his youth, and now in his memories, nothing so dominated Mel's life and mind as did the restaurant his father and uncle had co-founded.

They had been in the catering business together for years, working weddings, bar mitzahs, company picnics, private parties and the like, and all that was to continue while their primary concern would be the establishment and development of a rather pretentious "continental style" (and not kosher, thank you) restaurant in what had previously been a roadhouse drinking establishment that, for some historical reasons he can no longer remember, already bore a name they chose to keep: "Townleys."

Surely the name stemmed from an Anglo-Saxon settler in Elizabeth, and the naming was all part of an upward mobility ploy, an effort to climb that came all too late for my dad and his brother, Al, at a time when so many other Jews around them had already done the job. But this was their time, finally; this was their great effort to make it as others had done, and others around them would fail to do, so that it was their fate to try here and now or fail forever.

The site of their great enterprise was set on a broad knoll rising from the sidewalk in the front with ample parking in the rear alongside the tail end of an old Italian neighborhood, and then on the other side an expanse of lawn rising up from the curb and leading toward an extensive woods that would some years later become the grounds of a new university between Elizabeth and Union just south of Hillside.

It was here that Mel's father and his brother set down their rock, here his mother, his sister and eventually he came to work, both on the main first floor dining area and the party room above and then in the basement, then beyond a storage area and baking pantry in the fully-equipped Kosher catering kitchen by means of which the shadow of the restaurant's Jewish side spread out to the synagogues and homes, dining halls and picnic grounds in the towns and townshps that made up the broader Elizabeth-Newark urban and suburban post WWII world.

Mel's father worked day and night; and as the business ran into its early problems, his mother came to work there as well. Sometimes and increasingly as she finished high school and started college, his sister worked there too, although her main job was to babysit for Mel until, he at age nine, she, age nineteen, married and escaped restaurant, college, parents and brother—all of them—at once. As for Mel, a young man named Arthur became his babysitter until it was clear he needed no one, so he was left to his solitude and undisciplined eating from fifth grade through senior high.

The restaurant then was the context for his lonely evenings, his early life musings, his growing sexual fantasies, his homework and his first efforts at writing. The restaurant consumed his father and his father consumed food, so he was the massive hulk Mel feared and was ashamed to introduce to friends, thus exposing the sources of his own over-weighted being. The restaurant and his father left him virtually motherless in relation to a woman often too shy to express her feelings—at least until later in his life.

The restaurant was the source of shame for his sister, because its very existence revealed the family's not quite having made it status; that she had to work there while the other teenage girls in her postwar group did not, was a continual, festering sore in her young life, especially if a friend and family came in and saw her standing in as cashier or whatever. In the great snowfall of 1947, Elaine walked from the restaurant all the way down Elmora Avenue all the way over to Canton Street and up to our house near Warinanco Park, with the snow falling down and piling up to way above the top of where her nylon-stockinged legs disappeared into her long boots. Her lips turned blue, her legs blue. She almost collapsed into our apartment, falling to the floor and crying beyond control with her mother preparing the bed and she herself swearing in a near scream that she would never work in that restaurant again.

In fact, she never did. Her mother turned against her magician neer-do-well boyfriend, and after some weeks of forlorn mourning, she met the man she was to marry at a YMHA dance. She dropped out of Upsala College, married, and never took another college class or held a job again in her life—although she would one day coordinate the compilation of a cookbook, California Kosher, that was a big hit in every synagogue and Jewish gift shop throughout the country. Such was the effect of the restaurant.

As for Mel, the restaurant was the source of loss and shame, but also the forging of his own identity, especially after Arthur ceased to babysit him. Over the years it became his source of work and wealth, providing the monies for his theater and jazz events, his first car and even his first tentative efforts in love. Of course he hated working there. The catering jobs were fine enough, except when some of his prospective girlfriends appeared on the scene. But in the restaurant, he was the hat check man, the busboy, the third string dishwasher and mop up man, and nothing humiliated him more than seeing his father hobnob with guests, introducing him as his proud heir and lauding his accomplishments to the sky.

It hurt him to watch his father cater and yes pander for his clients. He hated his father's ethnic jokes, his off-color forays, his back pats and guffaws. It all seemed so rotten and wrong.

The only restaurant job he took on that seemed half-right was his role as amateur lawn mower and planter. Here his father showed his more poetic and earthy side—the small city Jew alienated from the earth who loved to make beautiful patterns of flowers and shrubs to enhance his lawn and set his restaurant in a kind of bucolic quasi-Anglo splendor. Lord of his estate (Townley's sounded just right). Mel's father taught him how to mow on a slant, how to plant and care for all new flowers he had at his disposal. He worked alone on Saturday mornings and then shifted into his hatcheck or busboy uniform. He went down to see if the baker had been sober enough to bake all he was supposed to, to see if his uncle Benny, his Aunt Dot and their Black assistant Ernie had done all they were supposed to do for the party that would take place later that afternoon. He sat at the bar talking about art and golf with his uncle Al, his father's partner, they used to call Izzy (was he?) who looked sadder by the day.

Above all, he loved schmoozing with the waitresses: Ruth, the mother of a young Yale professor who wrote of Sartre and Camus, while she worked away at the job that had supported him through all his graduate work; Olga, the beautiful European hostess, who'd escaped the Holocaust and seemed to be waiting for the right eligible bachelor (why couldn't it be he?) to come in to the dining room. Then, finally there was Mrs. Rubin, a woman approaching 50 but whose beautiful tightly braced breasts gleamed out from her low-cut white and sometimes sheer blouses which were not quite covered and indeed seemed to strain out of her svelte black jackets. How often he masturbated over the one woman and then the other.

How terrible when Olga met her husband-to-be, and then it was all Mrs. Rubin who seemed to lean over to let Mel see her breasts as she said, "Hello Mel, what a man you're becoming," in a horsey voice that seemed a welcoming call to bed. Sometimes he would have to deliver things to her apartment, and he would ring the bell holding his breath, till she opened and took what he brought, with her giving him a little kiss of thanks that all but took his breath away.

"Too bad you're not just a little older and not Dorothy's son," she once said, and he could smell a slight scent of liquor on her breath. That night his erection seemed to burst open as he had the most painful and exquisite orgasm as he lay in bed.

But none of his restaurant adventures and fantasies equaled the times when Townleys burned down. The first time he was awakened at three in the morning as his father received a phone call and woke wife and son to race with him over to the restaurant, as the firemen sought to put out a fire they could only contain after the building had all but burned to the ground. All of us cried as our labor and dreams blew up in smoke, and as we wandered through the ruins in the ensuing days sorting through the rubbish for salvageable odds and ends.

Meanwhile at school, his classmates mocked and jeered away, congratulating him on an insurance bonanza, speaking of vacations in Florida and the Caribbean, while all the workers awaited their unemployment benefits which took so long in coming that many had to jump ship and find other jobs, while many of the customers got used to attending rival venues. Mel couldn't stand all the jokes and rumors and innuendos; he defended his parents to the limit, but at the same time had his doubts as well. Meanwhile he tried to help his father going over the inventory of things lost, lending his ear for the plans to rebuild the restaurant in ways that would make it bigger, better and yes, more fireproof.

It seemed that the fire had resulted from a faulty electrical connection with flames shooting up from the catering kitchen to and through a wooden floor that served as kindling that in turn converted a minimal spark into a raging blaze. So now the new floor would be of some kind of inflammable liquid compound that would gradually harden into a rubberish finish easy on the workers' legs and yet beautiful for all the customers to see and feel. Then too the new ceiling of the restaurant was of that special fire-resistant material that sound-proofed and beautified all.

The plans in motion and the work begun, Mel's father and uncle took the opportunity to alternate some vacation time, with the father seeming to heed his schoolmates' suggestions by heading south through the Carolinas and all the way down to Miami Beach, so that Mel's first and only trip down the east coast from Elizabeth to southern Florida was again the product of the restaurant which ruled his family's life.

What a pleasure going that long way, his father at the wheel and him trading off with his mom in the co-pilot seat and the backseat as they made their way south. It was summer so the air conditioner was king, and Mel was thrilled even when bored by the country and western radio music, the local chit chat on the airways and time and again Arthur Godfrey playing his ukulele and singing of Florida oranges.

Three days driving, and staying at Triple A motels, they finally checked into the Hotel Raleigh, one of the smaller art deco hotels near the major beach venues. Off they would go to Wolfie's for deli diner. But during the day, he left his parents to their own devices as he made his way first to the swimming pool and then to the beach, where he met up with a young girl, twelve like himself, virtually breastless, though nubile, who loved to do daring flip flops in the water and come up brushing against his legs and genitals until the sport turned into the earliest sex game of his life—one that went on for hours with squeezes and kisses as they explored their awakening bodies and desires. After some days, however, the girl's love talk grew more intense; and he found himself embarrassed to be seen by other beach girls walking and playing with a breastless wonder while they all but flaunted their more developed forms before his anxious eyes.

Unable to win any of these other girls, he no longer wished to play with the girl he was winning, preferring to swim out from the shore and tread water in an area where she couldn't find or reach him. So it went for the last few days of his stay, as he imagined the poor, rejected girl searching the beach for him, while he treaded water avoiding jellyfish and man ray, but above all avoiding her, until his father signaled he'd received a call from his brother urging him to begin the long road back because the rebuilding project now required their agreement on delicate matters. So he left the girl behind and happily made his exit, happy to head up the road and forget her forever, though he never really did, happy to stop a day in Washington to see Abraham Lincoln's monument, the White House, Congress and all the wonderful buildings, and then, make it back the next day to New Jersey, to see the wondrous new restaurant that had made this trip possible and was now advanced enough to reveal how much better it would be than the old one it once was.

How wonderful and elegant it looked now, inside and out, and how magnificent the lawn and flowers that beckoned him for trimming and enriching. Suddenly all the resentment he had felt toward the restaurant faded, as he realized how much it was the source of his aloneness and inner self, but also the outer façade he would often use to face the world—how much the restaurant was laying at least some potential groundwork for his going to college and possibly going beyond, providing the bases for his life.

The restaurant reopened, gradually most of the workers and customers returned, all going well, and Mel was back to work both in the restaurant and the catering kitchen, happy now to win the money he would need for his future life. All seemed well until he sensed his father getting in some kind of trouble with some of the shadier types who frequented the restaurant so that Mel, now resentful, began hanging out with his friends at the nearby White Castle or—his great new love—a nearby Italian restaurant, avoiding his family's restaurant as much as he could given the fact that he still had to work there even as his friends went to the new Jewish country club, even as they partied and petted while he worked in the kitchen or served as busboy at one obnoxious party or another. All this until one day, enraged by one boorish customer, he poured a pitcherfull of water not into the customer's glass but the space between his fingers, so it went all over him, his father racing across the room to prevent the customer from punching his son out, separating him from the customer and virtually thrusting him out of the restaurant, telling him the words he wanted to hear—that he would never work there again.

A few years later, one night, the restaurant burned down again—not so severely as the first time, but enough so that things stopped again for some months. In the second hiatus, his father had time to go with him almost nightly, driving through the Lincoln Tunnel and heading across Manhattan to the trotters and pacers at

Yonkers and Roosevelt raceways, where they won time and again, building up the kitty that would suffer constant reductions from all those nights of jazz, theatre and failed love in his late teens, but would still be enough (with more help than memory allows him to admit) to at least partially finance his one year in an ivy league college.

But even after that first college year, and yes, even after his father's gambling addiction forced him to sell out of the business and move himself, wife and son to California, installment payments from the restaurant helped to fund Mel's continuing education for years into the future. The restaurant he hated had shown Mel the east coast from Miami to Maine; it had helped him in junior high, high school and then college; it turned out to be the truest foundation of his life.

The Magic of Memory

Now it is done. Now the story ends. And there is no way to tell it. The art of fiction is dead. Reality has strangled invention. Only the utterly impossible, the inexpressibly fantastic, can ever be plausible again. Red Barber, "Miracle of Coogan's Bluff" (from the *New York Herald Tribune*, October 4, 1951)

They told him that it would be the culmination of his Jewish education and would crown his entrée as a young man into his community. And surely the days from March 1951 until and beyond his Bar Mitzvah on January 12, 1952, marked the most crucial period of his adolescence. Of course, for many people in his town, and for many others as well, the most memorable days were those of the three plane crashes within a period of two months that made Elizabeth and its nearby airport known throughout the world. Everyone talked of the problems of Newark Airport, but the residents of Elizabeth all knew that the airport was really in our town; and the fact that buildings were hit and pedestrians killed here seemed to confirm their entitlement, filled them with a perverse sense of pride and of course some guilt over the pride that, try as they might, many of them just couldn't shake off.

The first crash was on December 16, 1951, the second on January 22, 1952; the third of February 11—with a composite death toll of 119. Of course, no other sequence of events could match it. And even some sixty years afterwards, Judith Blume, the town's most famous writer, mainly known for her portrayal of young adult women, finally novelized the crashes and their lingering effects on some of the Jewish families in the town.

Mel of course could never forget the sequence either, and he remembered especially the speech the rabbi of the synagogue closest to the airport (The Temple) made one Friday sabbath night, about the crashes and those who profited from the limited regulations which made the airplane companies so rich and such unimaginable accidents so possible.

However, truth be told, the crashes were never to have the same place in Mel's memory as did other matters occurring in that time period. There were two over-riding matters that weighed heavier upon him and yes, his family. The first, of worldwide importance, was the Rosenberg trial, which, begun and concluded in March 1951, dragged on with appeals and controversy in the many months that were to follow. And yes, the second event of course, standing above all, had to be his Bar Mitzvah.

Mel remembers these two matters and wrote stories about them later in his life. But what always stays with him, what stands etched as a special and even magical moment of his young life, occurred on October 3rd, 1951, just five-plus months after the Rosenberg decision, just two-plus months before the first plane crash and just days more before the second. And what was this event? The day he and the Giants beat the Dodgers in a decisive pennant playoff game culminating in a walkoff homerun.

He and the Giants, because there is little doubt about his part in the wonderful victory. To be sure Don DeLillo wrote pages and pages about the homerun; but, for all he did with such majesty, DeLillo failed to register the magic which Mel practiced and which won the day.

To be sure too, he missed most of the game because they played while he was at school—which perhaps explains why the Giants were losing. But he remembers racing home to his apartment, opening his door and turning on the tv set to find that his team was losing 4-1 and it was the bottom of the ninth!

It was then that, with terrible grit and determination, Mel grabbed a much-used red, tomato-shaped plastic ketchup dispenser (luckily it was empty) and began playing one of his favorite house sports with what served as a fungo ball: taking his bat and hitting the plastic tomato against the aluminum Venetian blinds next to the tv set (the aluminum giving in to the ball's impact, so there were no hard rebounds and the ball could be quickly retrieved after each shot).

Mel could now set the rhythm of his tosses and swings to the progress of the inning. Or, is it more correct to say that he set the progress of the inning to the rhythm of his moves? DeLillo tells us nothing that helps to settle this question.

Here were the Giants, tying the Dodgers after trailing them all year long, and now trailing them again in the bottom of the ninth of the third and final playoff game. And here they were up against a team marked by two great Black stars, Jackie Robinson at second and Don Newcombe on the mound—a new generation and race of players ready to take their place in the sun, but here to be stymied in probably the darkest day and worst moment of their Big-League lives. Mel had become a Giant fan because Sid Gordon, the Jewish home run hitter was the team's third baseman some years earlier; and then, long before the famous homerun shot, his worship had transferred to the non-Jewish center-fielder Bobby Thomson. But by '51, Hank Thompson, Monty Irvin and above all the amazing Willie Mays came along (years later Orlando Cepeda would follow) to push Thomson out of the outfield and into Gordon's old position and thereby further change all Mel's Giant identifications. Bobby was really on his way down as a hitter, so this was his last great chance to come through; he was no doubt Mel's last but already fading white hero. But he was about to have his one truly shining moment before he hung them up, and Mel would do all he could to make that moment shine, even as Willie waited on deck for a chance that was not to be his that day.

But what a chance this was for Mel and Bobby because the plastic tomato ball made a great blasting sound when hitting the blinds and yet the ball went dead on contact for an easy pickup and second fungo as quick as anyone could imagine.

All was set as Mel lined up with shortstop Alvin Dark and Newcombe threw the ball, whenMel hit his tomato against the blinds, just as Dark singled and landed with Mel on first base. Mel hit the tomato again as first baseman Gil Hodges moved to the right and lefty Don Mandrake the Magician Mueller joined with Mel in a single against the blinds just to Hodges' left and into right field. Next came Irvin batting cleanup, and Mel for some reason missed hitting the ball, causing Irvin to foul out. Hopes began to fade. But then came that other good old lefty, Whitey Lockman and boom! He and Mel launched a slicing fly to left-center field, making the blinds rattle, with Dark scoring, but, with Mel struggling to pick up the tomato, Mueller jammed his ankle as he slid into third and was forced to leave the game. Lockman got to second all right; but with all the anxiety he suffered as Mandake went toward the lockers, Mel went to the fridge for a can of 7UP; and in retaliation, with men on second and third, Dodger manager Chuck Dressen summoned Ralph Branca in to relieve Newcombe, with Mel sipping his drink during the pitcher's warmup.

Now Branca was known to be half Italian but he was also half Jewish, with some of his relatives dead in Auschwitz and other camps. To this day, Mel has considered a sign of the universe's injustice and indifference the fact that Branca was to be known for the rest of his cursed life for what was to happen in the next few seconds. And Mel saw himself somehow implicated in his sad fate, which it must be said, the damned pitcher always accepted with more grace under pressure than a Hemingway hero.

Up stepped Thomson, the flying Scotchman and Mel's no-longer favorite player now in his fading phase. Still, looking fantastic, tall and majestic with his new lean-over stance, more like Stan the Man Musial than Joltin' Joe Di, Bobby menaced Branca as he eyed him and tilted his bat in the pitcher's direction. But with Mel taking a time out to toss his soda can, Branca snuck in a perfect strike that left Mel smarting. Put on the alert, he now concentrated all his energies, his muscles tensing as Branca went into the stretch and Thomson readied for the pitch, which the righthander rifled toward Thomson's cocked bat just as Mel tossed the plastic tomato high up in the air, and just when it came down and in, both Mel and Bobby and Bobby and Mel wacked their incoming pitches with all their might deep into the clattering Venetian blinds and the left field stands of the mighty Polo Grounds with such explosive force that Boom! Boom! the crowd roared and it seemed as if lightning struck and music blared as the billboard seemed to explode and the world came unglued (*There's a long drive ... The Giants win the pennant, the Giants win the pennant, the Giants win the pennant, ... I can't believe it! I can't believe ...*) so that, as they both rounded the bases like Robert Redford in *The Natural*, with fans screaming and teammates joining to loft them on their shoulders, the combined impact of plastic tomato and ball came to resound collectively and immortally as "the shot heard around the world."

Afterwards, there was talk of sign-stealing. But when not? And if it were so, how much more awful was it for the Holocaust-cursed fall guy who was duped and made to eat humble pie in a phony pony show set up by his key duper. But in all of the back and forth, no one mentions the truly decisive story, about a Bar Mitzvah-bound boy bashing his plastic tomato-shaped catsup dispenser against the Venetian blinds in a lower middle-class house in Elizabeth, New Jersey as the Giants indeed played catchup. If anyone stole any signs, it was probably Mel—something no one has mentioned. But now you know.

The Brothers Weiskopf, The Circle, and the Rosenbergs

1.

I've heard it said that unhappy dissident Russian Jews in the 19th Century divided in choosing Zionism or socialism as their solution to the so-called "Jewish Question." Zionism meant Herzl and socialism probably meant Kautsky or Bernstein or, by the 1900s in Russia, a man, now all but forgotten, by the name of Julius Martov. Eventually some of the socialists turned to Lenin while others did not. Later some of the Leninists would follow Stalin, while others went with Trotsky. And so it went…

I'm not sure any of this is true or fully accurate but it seems to explain, partially at least, some of the things that happened to my father's family way back when. Of course it doesn't maybe explain that letter I wrote and sent about the Rosenbergs, and all the stir it caused. But who could explain that? I'm not sure I can do so fully even to this day. All I know is what I know. Maybe someone else clued into what happened may be able to figure it all out.

We can start with the fact that when the Weiskopfs left Russia, some went to London, maintained their probably fictitious Russian family name and quickly got involved in the Third International politics which they saw as the logical and legitimate heir of their Second International affiliation. So indeed, they became members or fellow travelers of the British Communist Party.

Meanwhile other Weiskopfs landed on Ellis Island, where some had their names changed to Weisman and others didn't. The Weiskopfs who kept their name seemed to maintain the leftward leanings that corresponded to their pattern in Russia, while those who became Weisman and thus automatically more American, placed their hopes in the Democratic Party, especially as it was personified by FDR and other Liberal anti-Communists.

Almost all the Weisman family members escaped the Jewish CP cauldron of New York and settled in and around the more Jewish areas of Newark; then most of them gradually shifted out of those areas with the richer ones white-flighting up to or near the Oranges and the somewhat poorer ones ending up in or around Elizabeth. Mel's paternal grandfather made the latter shift, but with his father, especially during the Depression, it was clearly back and forth between Elizabeth and Newark, and sometimes Manhattan or Brooklyn (even Coney Island) until he and his brother Al moved to the Elizabeth area more or less for good. There they maintained family ties with the Weiskopfs, but there was always a sense of difference. The Weiskopfs and their allied families, the Barons and Abrahams, seemed more intellectual and left wing than the Weismans, who more fully maintained Jewish affiliations, traditions and beliefs and cultivated a vague and inconsistent liberalism that would sustain their separation from the Weiskopfs intellectually and in other ways as well.

Max Weisman, Mel's grandfather, was a heavy drinker and the most Russian member of his family. A provisioner in the Tsar's army, he was always on the outs in his community and committed suicide in 1936, apparently because of some shady business deal that went awry. His abused wife, my grandmother, apparently couldn't bear to lose him nevertheless and died the next day, at her husband's funeral. With that, my father then took on all more officially the position he'd already held as virtual head of the Weismans. He apparently felt the need to help his younger siblings, to become financially solvent and in the process learned how to be the leader of his family as well as of the community in which he lived. The loss of his parents, and a pre-war lull in the Depression, combined with my mom's biological clock fed decisions that led to my conception. I don't think I was a mistake, though after I wrote the letter some felt that I deserved to be after all.

Anyway, the patriarch on the Weiskopf side was my grandfather's brother, his uncle Morris, another heavy drinker who nevertheless maintained the leftist inclinations of the New Jersey Weiskopfs and their cousins. My father respected his uncle and the whole Weiskopf wing of the family. But more important to him was his close friendship with one of Uncle Morris's Weiskopf nephews Martin, or Kelly as he was somewhat mysteriously called—a man who started as a Kosher butcher, but whose talents led him to become a concert singer, and whose political leanings kept him bound to the CP.

By comparison, my father was too smart to be tempted by old world-style politics, paid his Democrat dues, and focused on his business. How these two could be such deep friends was beyond reason. But that friendship, more than anything else, was what kept the two wings of the family together. And the real point here is how, for so long the differing politics of the Weiskopfs and Weismans, despite Depression, War, Cold War and me, failed to destroy what little there might have been of cohesion between these related families and in fact would provide a framework that would keep the family together, at least for a while. And strange as it may seem, my scandalous letter that almost tore my family apart also then served as the added glue binding them together at least for some years after.

2.

The first blow to our family's flimsy cohesion came before I was old enough to remember, when many loyal Communist Jews felt betrayed as Stalin signed his infamous non-aggression pact with Hitler. True, many members knew of the purges of 1936 when a grand number of high-profile Jewish Bolsheviks were exiled or executed, with of course Trotsky ridden out of the party and into the Mexican exile which led to his death. Jewish writers and artists were to go—including Isaac Babel, the one who I got to read pretty early along my road. And of course many other writers and politicians could be named. However, what most disturbed the most

Communist of my Communist relatives was this pact which, according to one of the Abrahams, gave Hitler and Stalin too a free hand in dealing with the Jews wherever they found them. Of course, some family leftists actually justified the pact as a strategic one giving Stalin more time to build up his war production base and his army. And many stayed in the party still grumbling and fearful for what might happen to relatives in and near the Soviet Union.

After Hitler broke the pact and declared war on the Soviet Union, the CP embraced Browderism, with its great and shocking project of building a popular front between CP members and "progressive Democrats" along with even less progressive factions who stood against Germany during the war. In this sense, Browderism helped unite the left in our family and form at least a provisional bridge between CPers and Roosevelt-loving liberals.

Seizing the moment, my father urged all Weismans and Weiskopfs to join together in what he called "a family circle." Here, despite their differences, family members could keep in touch and build deeper ties especially among the kids, so that they would know, and even love each other as time went by, so that maybe they could help even U.S. family members still in need and help others still in Europe if they wanted to come to the U.S. All the family members agreed it was a wonderful idea, and they began having planning meetings culminating in the first family reunion of 1945, just as WWII was coming to an end.

How could I forget at least some things from this gala event? It seemed that every Weisman, Weiskopf, Abraham and Baron and whoever gathered together in what was a synagogue rented for the occasion. I remember especially when my father fumed at Rabbi Feitz for not renting his hall for such a secular and perhaps somewhat radical cause. Here, Mel knew, was the seed that would send his father from the orthodox synagogue of the all-powerful Ralbi Feitz to the more middle-of-the-road (and Zionist) but initially poor synagogue of Rabbi Golub. But in the meantime, he was happy to get a hall Rabbi Golub arranged for his fledgling group.

Sure enough, the day was a great one, as family members gathered from all over New Jersey and even New York, as they came in from South Orange, Newark, Hillside, Bayonne, Jersey City, Staten Island, Brooklyn, the Bronx and who knows where else? Everything began with lots of hugs and kisses and presentations to the young ones of old timers they'd never heard of, but also their offspring more or less the same age as the young Weismans. The hellos continued with hors d'huevres and drinks. And finally, Mel's father took the podium and began reading off a tedious agenda. There were items about dues and the need for a treasurer, about future projects and trips. And then came the parade of kids, each costumed as if it were Halloween or Purim or some such event. He, dressed as a farmer, with farmer's hat and pitchfork, a plaid shirt and overalls, a corncob pipe in his mouth, sang out ''Oh what a beautiful morning, oh what a beautiful day.''

And then there was the great Jewish lunch with all the trimmings, and then his father gave the keynote speech about the need for the Family Circle to keep us united, to help one another grow and thrive in the postwar years. Then he broached a serious point about the group being above politics and never lending itself to a divisive cause that could break the group up—because family had to stand above all.

Mel could only understand a small fraction of what his father was saying. And it was only then that he heard some protests, some snickers and nay-saying that came mainly from the Weiskopfs more or less seated together with those Abrahams and Barrons who were present.

This exclusion of politics was ridiculous, said one, "as if the support for a Zionist Israeli state weren't political or wouldn't have serious political repercussions." How could you keep politics out at this crucial time, with Europe in ruins, the concentration camps opened, the Nuremberg trials in progress, and the fate of Jewry and the world itself at risk?

Still my father persisted and prevailed at least for a time. Whatever were the political views held by different members, we as a group had to stick together through thick and thin; and most of the Circle members applauded, though it was clear that the lack of unanimity would eventually spell great trouble for this Circle.

Of course things went well for some time, with several events where some cousins helped me act out a play I'd adapted from a story by Nelson Algren, and I even became secretary of the young cousins' group, working up a couple of newsletters that announced achievements among the kids, and events they'd planned, going to the Museum of Natural History or a baseball game in New York— things like that.

But as the Cold War deepened, conflicts in the Circle bubbled to the surface, first of all because some of the Weiskopfs wished to use some of the surplus in the Circle budget to help rebuild mother Russia, while at least some of the Weismans wished to use the surplus to help the state of Israel—to plant trees in the Negev or wage war against the Palestinians and other Arabs. Some thought the circle could support both causes, but others wondered about the deeper rift between Communism and Zionism, which had its main support in the Capitalist world.

3.

Strangely enough it was the Rosenberg case that brought the two sides together and avoided the early collapse of the Circle. For though some opportunistic Jews urged for the conviction and sentencing of the Rosenbergs to show how truly American they were, still almost of the Weismans agreed with the Weiskopfs and most of U.S. Jewry in smelling anti-semitism and the use of this one case as a means of attacking any and all of the many Jews who had had left-of-center beliefs and affiliations in the 1930s and 1940s. When the Rosenbergs were given the death sentence, almost all

Jews smelled the old antisemitic stench. So that all those in the circle had their own united front in opposing what they considered an attack on their people.

It was in these circumstances that, troubled and confused by the Rosenberg case, I wrote the briefest letter that horrified Circle elders and which would haunt and harry me for the rest of my life. Because I wrote a one-paragraph letter *to The New York Daily News* in which I stated that while I was a Jew, I was also an American and as an American Jew, I believed that if the Rosenbergs had committed treason they must die.

Why had I written such a letter, I wonder to this day. Was it to show off? Was it an expression of my growing exasperation at being Jewish and having my identity largely determined and pigeon-holed by that fact? Was I attempting to inflict damage on myself or my family? I could not, and still can't, answer such questions. All I knew was that I felt good, virtually liberated when I wrote my pithy note. And all I knew is I felt imprisoned by the letter once others had read it and began to comment about it.

No one was more horrified by my foolish and dreadul letter than the other Weismans, who expressed their outrage that a son of one of theirs had so declared this shameful position and thereby threatened the union of the Circle itself. My father was so livid, he could not talk to me. My Uncle Al, always so calm and wise, said he saw my little note.

"What did you think?" I said almost with a sense of pride.

"I think you should think about what you think before you send out a letter that might do people harm."

"But they're spies," he argued.

"Maybe yes, maybe no," said his uncle. "But they're going to kill them to set an example, and it's no accident that they're Jewish just like you and me. They killed six million of us in Europe, and now they're killing us here in the U.S. as well."

By this time, I have to admit that I kind of resented being Jewish and all the grief it caused me at school and in everything. I had begun to lose faith in the Jewish god, and that made it worse, because I found there were many Jewish atheists, but they were still Jews, as I was and as were the Rosenbergs. But now my letter was defining me as a self-hating Jew who had endangered the unity of the people and put all Jews and Jewry at risk.

And so it was that Mel's father insisted he attend the next board meeting of the Family Circle, literally dragging him to the meeting and offering him to be sacrificed as Abraham had done to Isaac so many epochs before. And so it was that Mel's father apologized to our relatives for his son's thoughtless and shameful act.

"I don't know what came over him, because this is not what we've taught him at home. But he's very young and I just thought he should have a chance to explain himself and listen to what we have to say, and maybe even apologize or do whatever we decide is right."

"I was so shocked by his letter," said his Uncle Sam, "and I am no lover of Communists Jewish or otherwise, but this is the kind of thing that can hurt us all."

"Mel," said his once-doting aunt, "don't you know that we are a people of justice. We are always for the underdog Jewish, Black or Brown."

"Many of us were misguided, many of us joined the Communist Party and other parties thinking that we could thereby somehow contribute to our fight for justice. Those who joined were wrong and many have left, and maybe even some of us were led to do what we did out of love for this country which has protected us, and which, under our great president, fought our greatest enemy."

"Come on," said a Weiskopf, "FDR betrayed us, he knew about the camps and executions and he did nothing."

"And what did Stalin do that was so great for the Jews?" said another relative. "Didn't he purge the Jewish communists? Didn't he exile and murder Trotsky, execute Zinoviev and Kamenev and who knows how many others?"

"And look at that shameful pact with Hitler. Wasn't that the greatest betrayal not only of Communism but of humanity itself."

"It gave Russia the time needed to prepare for war," said one Weiskopf.

"He beat Hitler more than FDR did," said another Weiskopf. "The Russian Communists saved what was left of European Jewry by winning the war, even more than did our U.S. troops."

"Plenty of young Jewish American boys lost their lives over there too," said still another.

"Yes, but it was the Russian army and Russian people—Jews and non-Jews—who did the heavy lifting," said Sophie Barron, one of the richest and simultaneously most fully leftist members of the circle, a card-carrying Communist from way back.

"And what are they doing now? Seducing gullible Jews to spy and kill for them, embarrassing us, damning us just so they can add to the numbers killed in the war."

"And now they're killing them in Russia and everywhere else," cried out my father's brother Ralph, who ran a liquor store with another of my father's brothers. "Voting to establish the State of Israel and then attacking Israel's 'Zionist incursion' as a way of winning Arab allies."

At that juncture, Uncle Morris, the acting family patriarch, spoke up, saying that my letter was in fact symptomatic of the Jew-baiting encouraged by the capitalist state, that I had been brainwashed at school and maybe at home, to hate my own people or any of the most progressive among them, that I should write an apology, and send it to *The Daily News*, and *The Daily Worker*, to boot, that I should write a letter of apology to the Family Circle itself which, as represented by this board, should show its opposition to the executions by donating money to the Rosenberg Defense fund.

And that was when I rose and said, "You can do what you like, and maybe I was wrong in my letter, but I'm not going to write any apology, I'm just going to—resign from the Circle. I quit," I said, surprised at my own words.

"You can't mean that," said his favorite aunt.

"Yes I can," I insisted. "And maybe we should all quit. Maybe we should stop trying to have a circle when we disagree about so much on all that's happening to us as a people, and when the Jews establish their state by doing the same thing to the Arabs as others had done to them."

"I can't believe my ears," said his father, left almost incoherent—"that my own son should compare us to Hitler, that he propose the breakup of the very circle we have fought to forge and preserve and who attacks his own people in their search for asylum after the war in a land that was given to them in Biblical Times. I said we needed to keep politics out of the Circle and now I see it creeping in and ready to destroy us. Now I see that I've neglected the education of my son for the sake of developing our business. Now I see what can happen to our young people here in America"

"What's needed at this time is wisdom, " said one of the Weiskopfs "And now we find our president, so wounded by a son's thoughtless and I would say obscene letter and wounded too by this same son's callous defense of his actions, this son who asks us to liquidate ourselves in the name of his own immature and unworthy political beliefs. We need a new president who can heal the wounds, or we can't go on; we need a president focused on the key issues of our time, which is above all, the effort by the U.S. to destroy the world movement toward socialism and communism, including the socialist state we believe will emerge in the new Israel where Jews and Arabs will learn to live in harmony like brothers and sisters."

"Don't hold your breath on that thought," said a Weisman. "And why should Sam step down just because his son wrote a stupid letter?"

Everyone put motions on the table and everyone found a second, but none of the motions carried, and the meeting seemed on the verge of breaking up in disgust and frustration. Indeed, it seemed at first that I had achieved my principle though unconscious goal—to destroy the circle and liberate himself.

But then, wiser heads prevailed among the elders. "Well, at least we all seem to agree on one thing," said Uncle Morris, "—that we've got to fight against anti-semitism; we've got to stand with the Rosenbergs, because even if they were loyal to Russia and the CP, they did nothing more than others who aren't being set up for the death chamber."

"Yes, we've had enough of death chambers," said another elder.

"So, at least for this year, we're should give all our dues to the Rosenberg Defense team, come hell or high water. And as for this foolish boy, we shall just refuse his resignation until he has a chance to consult with his parents."

"And talk to his rabbi," said another.

"That too if necessary."

"As for me," my father added, "if my son won't write a letter of apology, I will, and I'll send it to *The Daily News, The Daily Mirror, The Daily Post* and yes, *The Daily Worker* in the name of the Circle, but also in the name of the father of a foolish son."

So instead of bringing about the end of the Circle, my ill-considered, self-serving and shameful letter produced the opposite result—at least at first and for some time to come, with the Weiskopfs and the Weismans putting aside their eternal dispute between Zionism and Communism and joining together to give considerable sums to defend the Rosenbergs and others (Jews and non-Jews) for their presumed leftist affilations and supposed actions as the 50s rolled on.

As for me, seeing the result, I felt the Circle elders should maybe thank me after all. Which isn't to say that the Circle didn't begin to break up, to meet less and then fail to meet as the old division reared its head in the course of the Rosenberg execution and the rise of McCarthyism. I would go on to break with my synagogue soon after my Bar Mitzvah; and then seven years later, I would leave the east coast for the west, and gradually lose ties with much of my east coast family. Once, before I left, however, I tried to date Linda Abraham, the prettiest offspring of the Weiskopfs, but she turned me down, even throwing my misguided missive in my face—as did a few other Jewish girls, so that maybe that's one reason why I'd eventually end up pursuing non-Jewish women for much of my life.

Over the years I turned out to be the most Weiskopf of all the Weismans, following my more radical relatives, participating in "progressive" causes and activities, including some in support for the orphaned sons of the Rosenbergs, Robert and Michael Meeropol. I even got to know them, and had a fund-raiser for them once at my house; but, though I was tempted, I never could get myself to tell them about the letter I had written so many years before and which by the way I never formally repudiated. Nevertheless, as strange as it may seem, it may well be that the letter was what in the end might have led me leftward.

The Bar Mitzvah and the Death of God

1.

Mel's father was a key player in founding the Elmora Hebrew Center, a conservative synagogue breaking with the fearsome orthodox patriarch, Rabbi Feitz, who seemed to control all Elizabeth Jews, even the more upper class, wealthier ones who flocked around "the Temple." His father also helped recruit the Rabbi who marked Mel's formative years from as far back as he can remember—Rabbi Theodor Golub, a young man who looked to Mel like a Jewish version of George Brent, a second tier Hollywood actor, with his well-formed upper torso and shoulders, his perfectly trimmed moustache, and a deep, resonant voice that seemed like that of God Himself on top of Mount Sinai.

Mel revered his rabbi above all for his eloquence and apparent religiosity; and as the only son of the man who gave him however modest a home in this town with a growing Jewish population overflowing from Newark, he seemed to receive special attention and sometimes even affection from the rabbi with the thundering celestial voice.

Of course, the early days of the synagogue were modest enough—in a small store front hall that served as a Hebrew lesson classroom during the week, a place of worship on Saturday morning mornings, Rosh Hashanah, Yom Kippur and Passover, and a wonderful Bible story-telling space for Sunday School. The hall had a tin corrugated roof common enough in the 1940s, painted the drabbest possible grey and with a way of deadening sound that only a voice like the rabbi's could overcome.

At first, Rabbi Golub was the jack of all Jewish religious trades—the leader of the daily service, the leader and cantor on Saturdays and the high holidays, the story teller on Sundays, the man who handed out and received the Rosha Shuna pledges of money toward the building fund (you couldn't write out out anything, but you could bend down the tab on a card whch indicated the amount you wished to give—$50, $100, up to $10,000—this Jew was a dreamer as well as a rabbi), and then as the full story of the Holocaust and then the founding of the State of Israel became the hot issues faced in our communities, he committed himself, his synagogue and his congregation to helping Israel which he convinced his parishioners was the real answer to all that so many Jews had suffered and died for.

The rabbi sometimes even had to double as the mashgiach, usually a rotten rodent of a man who sat around the kitchen watching for Koshereit violations while taking food bribes and thereby eating away half the profits a caterer like my father could hope to make. But yes, when this lower form of life was too drunk to get up in time for the Saturday sevices including bar mitzvahs and whatever and there was no one else around who qualified, Rabbi Golub filled the bill. And that meant for Mel, at least in his first years in the synagogue, that Mel's Hebrew and Sunday school teacher was almost his everything else.

There was no doubt that his forte was not as a Hebrew teacher. Like many others who taught their Jewish students how to pronounce

—their Aleph Bet Gimel Dalet (or "Olive, Beth, gimme a dollar," as us kids would have it) that we needed to do for our Bar Mitzvahs, he never taught us what anything meant. On the other hand, he was a marvelous, titanic storyteller who enthralled the students by his brilliant and dramatic retelling of all the biblical stories of the bible, no matter how sketchy and lacking those stories might be in their defined narrative form. Imagine the story of Adam and Eve in Eden, of Cain and Abel, of Abraham and Isaac, of Isaac and Rebecca, of Jacob and Essau, of Jacob and Laban, of Jacob, Leah and Rachel, of Jacob and his sons, of Joseph and his brothers, of Joseph and Potiphar, of Joseph and the Faroh, of Moses, the plagues and the 40 years in the dessert. All of these stories told with great detail and drama, each passion explored and elaborated until his listeners were overwhelmed by all they heard.

In Mel's case, as he approached his teen years, his great imagining was of Rachel at the well, she with dark black hair, as beautiful as Elizabeth Taylor in *Ivanhoe*. How many times did he hang a blanket over his high bedpost and a pillow under his body, rubbing against the pillow as he imagined himself holding and kissing Rachel-Elizabeth in his arms, kissing her lips and then her intimate zones, as his gyrations moved him toward what felt like an shattering electric shock and the explosive expulsion of something he thought might be Vaseline. As a variant he placed an electric heating pad between his pillow and pillowcase, turned up the heat and mounted the pillow which was somehow the most beautiful of all dark Jewish princesses who like Rachel would wait for him for seven years, and like Ruth would go with him wherever he went all the days of his life.

This and more Mel owed to the wonderful storytelling powers of the magnificent rabbi it was his good fortune to have as his father's chosen spiritual leader of this new synagogue. And how wonderful that his father's role in the Rabbi's good fortune led him to have a certain place for Mel in his heart. But only gradually did that image begin to erode, only gradually something rang false about his wonderful rabbi, something that led him to doubt and eventually lose his faith in the rabbi, his father, and the Jewish God who was central to a religion he felt himself beginning to doubt and deny.

2.

It was not too many years before the work of Rabbi Golub and congregational leaders like his father led to the establishment of a brand new building in a more upscale neighborhood and the little shul became converted into the Elmora Hebrew Center, now somewhat holding its own with Rabbi Feitz's othordox synagogue and the Temple nearest to the airport. The Center even included its own Kosher kitchen for which Mel's father and mother were often the contracted caterers, so that the growing prosperity of the synagogue also meant some financial advantage for Mel's family, and a source of jobs and money for Mel's teenage needs for date and partying money.

Indeed, the Center now prospered from the growing prosperity of its members, who were mainly the less successful Jews now beginning, in the post war years, to catch up with the families whose clothing, grocery, liquor, sportswear and appliance stores had brought them some base for economic success even as the depression of the 30s deepened. Now after the war, in a booming economy, those in-between Jews, Mel's father included, began to show signs of life, as they moved out of the poorer parts of Elizabeth into the wealthier area "up the hill," where the better off Elizabeth Jews had already moved.

The Center sat precisely at the dividing line between the richer upthehill and poorer down-the-hill Jews, and it was also the place where kids from the richer and poorer neighborhoods gathered for their classes—mingling but also parading their differences, as the richer ones spoke of their new country clubs and their ivy league college applications and the poorer ones envied their more upscale lives and dating possibilities, seeking revenge in small ways, by being more macho or brighter or anything that would make them more special than the kids who had been singled out as more special than they.

In the midst of all this, Rabbi Golub seemed to change. He bought a better home now up the hill with the successful Jews; he bought better suits which accented his broad shoulders and thriving physique. It got about that his two boys were troublemakers, using their father's prestige to make themselves out as hotshots, and of course the Rabbi took some blame for this as an over-indulgent, upwardly mobile father. Now he no longer conducted the Hebrew School classes or held his wonderful Sunday school sessions but jobbed these functions out to less adequate assistants, so that Mel and the other boys had much less direct contact with him.

The cantor he hired was operatic and titanic, but the Hebrew school teacher was a holocaust survivor who'd lost his entire family and was placed with the synagogue by the United Jewish Fund, to do a job he simply could not do—teach Hebrew. Hardly able to speak English, he could explain nothing, teaching the boys the sound of things but not the meaning of any word, frequently lost in class as he probably remembered unspeakable horrors. The woman who taught Sunday school classes just didn't have the knack, made dry straw of the stories and inspired no one to do anything. And now, the only contact they did have with the rabbi was as members of a team the rabbi formed of Youths for Israel (the YFI), a group whose primary function was to raise money for trees in the Negev or other projects (maybe even arms).

So, Mel and his Jewish friends separated themselves from their Hebrew Bar Mitzvah studies, to go door to door, apartment to apartment, and house to house, seeking to get donations for what all Jews called "the pushka"—one of those cardboard tube canisters with tin top and bottom, the top with a mouth-like slot for all the change and folded dollars that they could induce their neighbors to feed. Most of the Jewish residents were receptive, all primed to give, but even some of them and many Christians declined, sometimes cursing Mel and the others, complaining about Zionism, the exploitation of Arabs, and Jewish pushka pushiness in general. One even called out to him when he rang, "I've already given to the Hitler fund to get rid of the rest of you!"

Such attitudes made Mel nervous and he grew to deeply resent Rabbi Golub and the Jewish homeland for taking him away from the very story world of religiosity the Rabbi had instilled in him—his youthful awe of God and things holy—to put him in the position of having to go begging for a cause which, however good it might be for Israeli Jews, was probably quite bad for Arabs, who, he tended to believe, were as human as his own chosen people, and were now to be brushed aside because of the Holocaust and the international support for a Jewish homeland induced by the indifference to Jewish suffering throughout the war years. And now, suddenly, the pious lover of Sunday school stories, the Jacob who loved Rachel at the well and wanted to live a Jewish life, found himself a Jacob wrestling with the Angel of Death and finding his love for his Rabbi and his faith in the Jewish god draining away even as he moved down each and every hallway ringing every buzzer and begging for a Jewish state he no longer felt quite willing to serve.

3.

It was in the middle of this growing crisis that Mel, perhaps run down by the conflict raging within him, turned sick, vomited again and again, saw giant spiders running across his bed, and giant pushka cans rushing toward his head, as his temperature soared to 104 and his mother desperately called emergency. The crisis passed, but the doctor's diagnosis was pneumonia, confining him to the house for a period of no less than three weeks, which crossed into Passover and Spring break week so that he was to stay in the house for at least a month until he fully recovered, unable to receive visits from friends, or (to his great relief) even dream of going house to house and door to door during the entire period of his confinement.

Since his parents were at work in the family restaurant, and his own sister had moved away, Mel spent each day alone. Soon his sickness seemed to have disappeared, but his doctor insisted that he stay at home or risk a relapse. Alone in bed, he somehow began to write some kind of prose poem about a medieval peasant who suddenly realizes that his life is one of exploitation by a Church that has told him to accept his fate. This piece drafted, he wrote another about a religious teacher who fools his followers into believing the silly things he has to say. One prose poem after another came forth, and even a few experiments in poetry and fiction. Before he knew it, he had a whole notebook of small works and decided that he indeed wanted to be a writer.

Once deciding, he committed himself to writing something each day, and soon it occurred him to write a couple of essays—the first about genocide and the other about the role of religion and the question of the very existence of God. The first essay he thought was going to be about the attempted extermination of the Jews, but soon turned into an summary of several instances of genocide in the past two hundred years. The Jews were not the only victims, he noted, pointing out the persecution of variety of religious groups and other undesirables, but also noting that even if we focused on ethnic genocide, there were the efforts to liquidate Armenians, gypsies and others. The root of genocide was racism and a general fear of the other, he wrote; and even those victimized could themselves be or become racists, as in the case, he found himself forced to admit, of the Jewish attitudes toward the gypsies and Arabs—not to mention Ashkenazi attitudes to Sephards. Finally, he wrote about the overall genocide of African peoples through hundreds of years, and the participation of so many peoples, including some that were also victims, in the victimization and stigmatization of Africans. He wrote about the liquidation of Native Americans, about Chinese exclusionary laws, and the internment of Japanese Americans during World War II. And if that were not enough, what about the question of the Jews and Palestinians, a matter which made him tremble and suffer to his depths. A true and honest Jew, he argued, would oppose racism and exploitation by any people, including the Jews.

As if this first essay was not damning enough there was the second essay that went through the ins and outs of religion and the illusions of solace and community it offered with respect to a belief in an afterlife and the importance of man to God. Considering all he had learned of life and history up to now, he had to accept the fact that religion had led to constant wars and useless killings, and even genocides, and that considering the question of beginnings, the question of eternity, of evil and all the rest, one could only come to believe, however reluctantly (because who wished to bear the consequences?) that the only rigorously logical conclusion was that the horrendous evil of the world was so great that it could only be explained by the non-existence of He who supposedly made everything.

Looking over his writings, the pattern was all too clear to him—that out of his illness-induced solitude he was discovering who he was by writing down his thoughts; and in fact he was becoming the young adult his solitude, illness and writing had led him to become—a boy who could not believe in the special virtue of his own people and in the very existence of the god he had been led to worship.

Undoubtedly the holocaust and genocide in general played much into his conclusion, for he thought, if there was a god who had the power to prevent such human activity, how could one worship Him, sing His praises and build one's life around Him, as some of the Jersey Jews did with respect to their rabbi and synagogue. The holocaust was the proof of the non-existence of the very god Jews had worshipped—always a Cruel God at best, but now beyond words and all modes of representation: the unthinkable god of a horrendous world of meaningless suffering—a world in which there was no light from heaven. And so this boy in his thinking reversed the classical positions: If God is dead, then life has no meaning: when the lepers discovered there was no God, they poisoned the wells. But who would want such a god or such meanings in any event, when the truth was that it was good to be free—of meaning, of bullying community and God too—it was good and important to face life with no meaning and with no life after life—to accept these difficult realities and to free oneself, to make of one's one and only life all that one could.

But once he was convinced of his position, what could this young boy of this bullying community do? His first reaction was that there was nothing he could do but tell his parents of his beliefs and cancel their plans for a Bar Mitzvah. But could he be so cruel to them and their hopes and expectations? Hadn't he scandalized and perhaps damaged them enough with the letter he had written condemning the Rosenbergs? Could he now all but announce to the world that his parents had failed to bring him up properly so that this boy who was such a good student and perhaps even a promising young writer, would disgrace his family again? And what would that mean for Rabbi Golub, who had personally taken care of the boy's religious formation and had people even thinking that this boy, so taught and formed, might himself become a rabbi.

Mel thought of talking to Rabbi Golub, but now he no longer felt the confidence to do so. How could this man whose own standard of living seemed to have gone way up in relation to his campaigns in defense of the Jewish homeland really be the one to tell about his loss of faith and his passion for an authentic life in the face of the meaninglessness of existence?

Instead, he turned to Alan Paskow who for some time had become his closest friend because they shared a hunger for knowledge and for doing something important in their lives. He and Alan studied the Roman Empire and produced a grand chronology of the various Caesars, their conquests, and cruel absurdities (the chronology was rolled on to a paper towel tube that was inserted in a wooden box with a window through which you could read an entry). They used this box invention to present their findings about evolution, from Lamarck to Darwin and Wallace, Ernst Haeckel, Herbert Spencer and onto the Huxleys—with much attention to Julian—a project which perhaps prepared the way for the biological and specifically Darwinian emphases in Mel's essay on the non-existence of god. Then they worked on Bacon, Locke, Berkeley, Hume, and Hobbes spending hours together working through ideas, often confused but finding their way as Mel realized that Alan, like himself, no longer believed in God. They shared their beliefs, and one occasion, they even dared to induce some of their friends to join them in defying their religion by seeing who could jerk off first in a contest that left them all moist and joyful and then fearful and ashamed.

Now, their bonding all but complete, now that they both knew God did not exist, and that the best life was one which sought authenticity and truth in the face of the fact of life's ultimate meaninglessness, he asked Alan what he should do about his Bar Mitzvah.

Alan would end up an expert on Heiddegger and would one day suggest to the great philosopher's widow to her face that her own intense anti-semitism and support for the Third Reich might well have had something to do with her husband's affair with his attractive and brilliant Jewish disciple, Hannah Arendt.

But back then, Mel's friend surprised him by saying that he owed a debt to his parents and community even in the formulation of his heretical views, and that for the sake of his family's feelings, he should just make this one last time sacrifice of his personal authenticity on the altar of familial consideration. Did he really want to become the first known Jewish boy in the community to reject the ceremony that seemed almost at the center of that community's sense of meaning and continuity? Did he want really to bring such humiliation and stigma on himself and his family, and should not he, the boy who had written a letter condemning the Rosenbergs to death, not wish perhaps not atone, but at least somehow somewhat compensate for what could only be viewed as an action born out of a growing alienation from justice as well as community.

Given all this, should he not take on the rite of passage and subsequently confirm his rupture with the Jewish god and his assumption of a life of alienation from family, community and self as something he takes on as a Jew, something he only takes on after his certification and confirmation, as Christians would call it, something that would have more weight as an act of separation and self-definition in the name of a godless but authentic life.

4.

Mel was amazed at Alan's argument, but he decided that his friend had a certain point. And why indeed should he spoil this crowning moment for his parents? True, he had grown up virtually alone as they put all their life energies in the postwar/post-Holocaust world of Elizabeth to bring success and financial fortune that had eluded them throughout the Depression. They had not been able to visit him at summer camp on visiting days, but during the week when no one else was seeing their parents; after his sister's marriage, he was left virtually alone at home and became the latchkey boy who blasphemed the Rosenbergs and now had lost his faith in the god which gave meaning to their lives. But still he had to accept the fact that he loved them and could not in the last analysis bring himself to do what the most zealous aspect of his identity had been urging him to do.

And so Mel sacrificed authenticity for love and respect. He continued on in Hebrew school, learning to mouth the sounds if not the sense of Hebrew and, assigned the part of the **Haftorah** he would have to learn to lead that small portion of the Saturday service that was the basic requirement for the Bar Mitzvah ritual, he went about studying every syllable and every half-melodic sound that made up the substance of the passage he had to read before the Hebrew Center community and all his family members who would gather there ready to hear his words and then celebrate this key event of Jewish life in a party that would probably be the biggest bash especially given who the caterer was going to be.

And yet never, in the midst of his preparations, did Mel lose sight of the fact that all this was a charade and that the truth was the death of God and the alienation of all humans from any guarantees based on family and community. Returning to school after his pneumonia hiatus, Mel felt differently as he walked among his classmates. No one, except for Alan, knew of his new identity and the path his life would take. He continued to socialize with his friends even as Spring Break approached, and indeed the only friend he found himself distancing himself from, at least on the surface was the only friend who knew his truth and thus the only one he found difficult to be with.

Alan had told Mel that he didn't want any more obscene bathroom hijinks, that he just couldn't relate to the cruder, more fun-loving boys; Mel for his part, wanted to experience the social life that he had attempted to develop in summer camps and now sought to realize in spite of his continuing inner sense of things (that feeling which grew so strong on Canton Street near the park) and all that had attracted him to and then turned him perhaps away from Alan—that he was both deeply introverted and extremely extroverted—in/out, the oscillations of his days and ways as he passed through what might have seemed a fairly normal childhood,, but was not. He began to read secretly and ferociously becoming an avid reader even as he was a boy living his adolescent and teenage life. But he also followed baseball, football and all the key sports of his time. And what did he not hide as the days before his Bar Mitzvah drew ever near?

5.

Spring break upon him, and with an important assignment to work on, he rushed to round off all his history class readings about the French Revolution and then, almost without a plan, began drafting a story of the revolution that quickly turned into a short novel of over 140 pages. It was called *Usurp the Divine*, and most of his classmates who knew about it thought it was the story of some great king or potentate named Usurp. But in fact, it was the story of a young supporter of the Marquis de Lafayette who became increasingly alienated from his childhood religion and even his hero, as he saw the need to break with the myth of the Divine Right of Kings and give his heart to a revolution which then, perhaps because of its radical godlessness, becomes increasingly evil until it swallows the most passionate revolutionaries and the young atheist himself who, all too fittingly is led off to be guillotined as the novel draws to its melodramatic end.

The writing was far from impressive; the sequence of events was mainly cribbed from one-dimensional narratives of the Revolution, and the love affair between the atheist hero, Jacques de Nuvier and his religious love, Leonora, was far from the stuff of potential greatness. Yet the narrative told of a man who unlike Mel was true to his atheism even if meant losing family, love and life.

Completing the short novel and submitting it as his classroom project, Mel finished the school year and spent perhaps his last pre-Bar Mitzvah summer playing ball in the park a block from his house. Only in the fall, and really after "the shot heard around the world," did he return to the task of learning and practicing his Haftorah, which, bringing it to perfection over Christmas break, he was fully prepared to present, though against his own nurtured beliefs, as his passport to adult membership in a community of which he no longer wished to be a part.

6.

The days leading up to the holiest of days in the life of a young Jew were filled with his parents' preparations: the invitation list in which he had to participate, as he chose carefully all the girls and boys who would accompany him during what was supposed to be the most magical day and evening imaginable Then came the purchase and fittings for a new suit, shirt, tie, shoes and thallus, his input into the reception treats for the members of synagogue and the family guests, the menu and all the arrangements—the flowers, the photographer, the band—needed for the dinner party.

Meantime, there was the final polishing of his presentation, and the final doubts about going through with this ceremony after all. Over Christmas break, just days before the event scheduled for the second week in January, Mel's nerves were near the breaking point. The first plane crash in Elizabeth came on December 16th. And he had sudden tantrums and had to hole up in his room until the immediate crisis passed and he could return to the living room. Alone, his mind flooded with images of marvelous sexual encounters with movie stars, beautiful schoolmates and prostitutes he imagined meeting at one bar or another. His penis grew so chafed from the constant rubbing against hand and pillow that he had to purchase ointment over the counter risking the jeers of the pretty drugstore cashier who he assumed had figured out what the ointment must be for.

Finally, in the living room, he heard his father comment as it was not indeed his usual way, about the growing persecution of writers and actors, many Jews among them.

"The Jews are the real target," he reasond. "Most of the rest are just cover. Now it's Clifford Odets, John Garfield, Arthur Miller. And there's that bastard, Elia Kazan, who's already named some names and the word is, he wants to name everyone. And mainly they're denying everybody's rights left and right."

"Mainly left," Mel chimed in.

"Well, yes mainly left, maybe thanks to you and your famous letter," his father came back at him rather abruptly and bitterly. "And don't think I don't know about your Bar Mitzvah doubts, don't think you can walk out on this by moaning and groaning and jerking off. This is one time you won't do your parents in. If the writer of *Death of a Salesman* has to testify, so you have to read your Haftorah."

"But he won't name any names, he knows it would be wrong" Mel retorted.

"And you're going to do what you know it's right to do, and there's nothing more to be said about that."

Nothing more to be said, the matter settled for all times—and as Mel heard his sentencing, he felt somehow relieved. There was no use in protesting—it was to no avail. Nevertheless, he could not resist seeing himself standing on the podium, following the rabbi's pointer as they went through each passage of the Haf Torah, and then in the middle of it, the boy, on the brink of manhood, lifting his eyes off the printed page and making the most remarkable of commentaries.

"My fellow Jews, let me announce to you all that I believe in the beautiful breasts of your most beautiful daughters, but in no way do I believe in what was our and is now your but not my God. Let me say I oppose all forms of antisemitism and racism—even our own. But yes, I must tell you that in the name of authenticity in an empty world, I cannot in any way, shape or form, go through with this sham of a service. I cannot commit sacrilege against the beliefs you have the right to believe, even if I believe that one of the great lessons of the Holocaust was above all that the god who Jews had prayed to in all their tribulations and most recently, in Auschwitz, Dachau or so many other places we can name, as they were herded into the gas chambers, simply and purely did not exist. I don't seek to fight off your illusions and dreams, but rather I choose not to sully or disrespect them and therefore ask you to refrain from singing my praises and giving me those famous bar mitzvah gifts, I only ask you that you honor the sincerity of my convictions as I do yours, and simply excuse me from a proceeding what will only make a mockery of all you believe, and leave me with a stain of dishonor for the rest of my life."

However, of course, this was all a dream. The day came and the day went. The morning ceremony moved right along; and called to the podium, Mel reluctantly left his seat and climbed up to the beama, where he greeted the Rabbi, the new operatic cantor, and even his Holocaust-traumatized Hebrew teacher, and then stared out across a sea of faces including the parents of many of his school friends and all those of the Family Circle who did not boycott this event. He spotted so many cousins he loved or hated, so many of his schoolmates, some of them even sending signals up to him—as if, sensing his doubt and hesitancy, they wished to help him shore up his resolve. And finally, he saw his father and mother, and even his sister and who beamed with pride and only a slight glimmer of apprehension. And he knew he could not deliver the speech he had dreamed up but must indeed come across with his great sacrifice, as the rabbi pointed the silver pointer and he began to read, as so many thousands of Jewish kids did before and after him, including some others who may have had similar atheistic convictions as his own, and eventually conclude the requisite sacred writing which it was apparently not necessary to understand, let alone agree with.

And so it was and so it had to be. The rabbi gave a little speech of how proud and happy he was that one of his favorite Sunday school students and a warrior for Israel before he fell sick last year, had recovered and led one of the most beautiful, soulful Haftorah readings he himself had ever had the pleasure to hear. How proud and happy he was for this congregation, these parents, relatives and friends who had supported such a boy, how much he hoped that in the future as in the past, this boy would live up to his past promise of being, like his father and mother, true leaders in our struggle to build our synagogue and the Jewish community, and our struggle to leave holocausts, sufferings and, he added, false if well-meaning radicalisms behind as we worked to create the great state of Israel.

The ceremony over, Mel made his way toward the beautiful dairy and sweet tables his father had prepared. He drank a cup of schnaps, and then received congratulations from all who had attended, as they filled their plates and stuffed their mouths with pickled herring gefilte fish, with delicious pastries and coffee and yes more schnaps, as the morning ceremony came to a roaring close.

That evening the invited guests all gathered at the Center's dining hall, where a band played, all sorts of appetizers were served, and Mel joined his school friends and cousins in a huge head table of which he was the center. At a certain point, his father gave a talk and then it was his turn to thank his father, his beloved mother, his rabbi and all who were here this evening which for more reasons than they would ever know, he would remember to his dying day. Then came the dancing, the eating, the drinking, and at a certain point, Mel could not resist getting up and singing a Sinatra song from the new album of torch songs which marked the great singer's comeback after Ava and the rest.

He can remember little more of this evening, except a key moment when the rabbi and his family got up to leave and the rabbi took him by the shoulders, embraced him as he cringed, and told him that he hoped that his Bar Mitzvah was not the end of his relation to the synagogue and the great Zionist cause, that he would be waiting to greet him whenever he was ready to take on the new role he could now play. Mel thanked the rabbi and assured him he would stop by, knowing all too well that he never would.

He remembers how later that night, sitting at the dining room table with his parents they sorted through the presents and gelt he'd received.

"My god," said his mother, "it almost covers our expenses."

"Glad it paid off," he said with little acid or venom.

"It's for your college fund," said his father. "We're putting money in there whenever we can."

Mel himself was impressed by all the checks and cash. He even wondered if this was why he had gone through with it all, after all. Certainly, he sensed no spirituality arising from the stacks of checks and cash.

On his mother's death many years later, he inherited the albums of photos she had collected, including one book specifically labeled *Mel's Bar Mitzvah*. What a grand group of photos portraying the event and so many details he'd forgotten! There he was with his father and mother's friends and relatives and his own crowd of friends as well. There he was dancing with a girl or cousin friend, or with his sister; and, best of all, where he looked happiest, with his mother, her pride and joy radiating from every poure, and him smiling, enjoying her joy. There was his father more obese than Mel was to ever become. There he was standing between one uncle and aunt after another, and there he was with all his friends sitting at the head table.

Perhaps most striking was the photo of the magnificent hors d'oeuvres spread, with a mass of chopped liver shaped into a duck and a huge egg salad shaped into who knows what. Then, at the very end of the album was a wonderful photo of all the kitchen staff working this catering job and making sure everything was perfect. There amidst pots, pans, and trays of food ready for the serving, were so many people close to Mel in his youth but who were too busy serving his feast to be at the party in his honor. There was his Uncle Benny, his mother's brother, who always worked with and for Mel's father, and always treated Mel with love. There was his aunt Mayra, Benny's wife; and there was Mel's Uncle Al, one of his father's brothers and his partner—another uncle who treated him almost as if he were a son. And there was Carl, the first Black man Mel ever knew, and Ernie, Benny's right hand man, also African American, who supervised Mel in many a catering job, and some years later would teach Mel how to drive and other things as well. There was an older waitress Mel can't remember, and yes, he could see the head of the horrible one, the Mashgiak, watching every move in the kitchen, ready to call out some violation of Kosher laws at every turn. And there Mel was himself looking so much the Bar Mitzvah boy, with yarmulke and tallit, as if he were the young Hillel or whoever on his way to becoming a great Talmudic scholar. So reverent, so engrossed in his ever so religious and spiritual thoughts, his face more gaunt and soulful than at many other times before and after the taking of this picture.

Who would have guessed that this boy had denied God's existence and had once felt he should bow out of the most important moment of a Jewish boy's life? Who would have guessed what a traitor of the Jewish people is here presented? Who would sense that this was the very last time when he would pay any homage to the Jewish religion and the horrendous, vengeful and arbitrary god who ruled over and dominated his people? And who were his people? Those who were there? Or those who would be in his life in years to come? How would he live his life without the help of God? What would his life be? Would he or could he even amount to anything, he who falsified himself in his Bar Mitzvah, he who already before his thirteenth birthday had said no to Jewish life as he knew it. This Bar Mitizvah boy who was saying goodbye even as he said hello to the wider world.

Book Three. Teen Times (1954-1958)

Miss Murphy, Love and Liberté (1955)

Sometimes one day or even one short sequence of events on one day takes on the same weight or some special form of significance in relation to years of growing up and finding one's way.

In my case, I can vaguely remember a day in the early spring of my sophomore year in high school when my absurdly reactionary Irish Catholic French teacher, Miss Mary Murphy, received word from the French Consulate that our second year class had been selected as one of the three New York-area school French programs to participate in a ceremony on Bedloe's Island marking the anniversary of the gift of The Statue of Liberty, to the people of the United States. Miss Murphy was thrilled by this communication, which she announced as a great honor and surprise, and which I now know she must have moved heaven and earth to make a reality. Of course, she spread the word to all high school and Board of Ed. officials and to the press in Elizabeth, New York, and even that city she most reviled, Newark.

All through our near two years with her as our teacher, my fellow students and I had come to despise her in every way. Ours was an all boys' public high school, separated from the girls since the late 1930s because of what were rumored to have been some nasty gender clashes in our hometown's own version of World War II. And Miss Murphy seemed to be carrying on a year-by-year war avenging past abuses, giving her students the hardest tests and holding us to the highest standards of French usage, making us hate her as we spent hours and hours preparing for exams we were bound to flunk.

She berated and humiliated us one and all in class, singling out each one for our stupidities, and yet constantly choosing and only later rejecting a series of pets, who immediately earned the hostility of their peers, each student playing and competing viciously against the others, until we finally woke up one day and realized she was the true and constant source of our mutual backstabbing and discord. And all the time she praised every move and word of her emerging Irish hero, Senator Joseph McCarthy and always awarded the highest grades to those who wrote the best defense of anti-communist witch hunts and hunters in the most elegant French imaginable.

The truth was that the high scorers were almost always those who wrote the most eloquent ass-kissing right wing diatribes, while the other students sat glowering, complaining about her in every way, and agreeing of course that she was Miss because who wouldn't like to miss marrying Mary quite so contrary, that she was single because she was the most horrendous bitch in creation, that she had never been and could never be touched by the fertile force of semen because she was so sterile and so repulsive to any normal male member that it would inevitably whither on seeing or (heaven forbid) touching her infested privates. So they—or yes, I own up: we—wrote notes about her on public walls, made fun of her with obscene bathroom graffiti; we filled condoms with hot water and hung them on the ledge above her office door until one finally fell as she exited, so that a warm viscous fluid that was maybe water mixed with vaseline (but who knew for sure?) landed on her head and dripped down from the tip of her witch's nose and onto her clothes.

What was viscous only made her even more vicious, especially toward the minorities in our school, making little discrimination among Blacks, Italians, Jews, Poles, and now some Asians and maybe our one Latino, all of whom were third-rate Americans compared to the great Irish immigrants who had risen from the depths of misery (and yes that was true) to be church, ward and educational leaders—including our most brutal teachers, as well as foremen, firemen, policemen, aldermen, and the whole miserable political class in the great pecking microcosm of America which our oh so lovely town and wonderful school so perfectly replicated.

Somehow Miss Murphy's pro-Irish-Catholic sentiments made her a supposed enemy of the Anglo establishment and a defender of all things Gallic as well as Irish. And yet her anti-Anglo resentments did not succeed in making her less conformist to the overall system which the Anglos dominated through a series of ethnic surrogates. This my classmates and I knew even if we could not quite articulate it. We knew how she was always angling for special favors and recognitions with French authorities in the New York area that her teaching and politics did not merit—how she always wrangled tickets to the most boring French operas at the Met and operettas at the Paper Mill Playhouse, how she bored and abused her students into learning the lyrics of the most turgid and silly of French songs and the most trite, boring and stupid poems. Now we were stuck with Miss Murphy's latest folly. The French gift and the poem by that Emma Molly Goldberg Lazarus pointed to the great importance of us Others in the history of Anglo-America. But though Miss Murphy despised the Jews and almost every other slimey minority, she could only wreak with pride over how her knowledge of French and the French I-scratch-your-back/you-scratch-mine system had once again out-trumped her shanty town Irish roots and now taken her to the verge of God's heavenly mansion.

"Boys," she told us, "this special recognition we've received will in fact be outshone by the contribution we shall make at the upcoming ceremony out of love for France and our beloved United States. Each day, we are infiltrated by more and more new immigrants who come here hungry, dirty and poor; and by hook or by crook each day some of these people rise to great heights whether they deserve it or not. It is true that many unworthy immigrants arrive—people contaminated with Marxism, socialism, anarchism and other foreign ideologies, people who never learn to appreciate their new home. But we are going to show the officials who have invited us how we stand against all that is negative and how we back to the hilt leaders like Senator McCarthy so that our country is cleansed of riff-raff and subversives and we rise to our true greatness.

"The French government under the magnificent Charles de Gaulle, who is fighting radical half-breed scum in Algeria and Indo-China, has decided to reaffirm its gift of friendship to the United States of America made more than seventy years ago; and we will be there on Bedloe Island to sing our praises to France and our own great country. We will show them what Thomas Jefferson High School and its modest but glorious French program are all about!"

With that she pushed back her grey hair and tucked in her blouse, as she taught us to sing "The Marseillaise" and, as if we didn't know it, the "Star Spangled Banner."

"Boys," she said, "it's our job to sing the two great anthems of our two great countries. It's also our task to rise each time France and the United States are mentioned, and every time an official is acknowledged. So now practice, boys, let our voices rise in song, and let us stand when we should. Others will recite the Lazarus poem, other will jump through hoops for all I care, but this is what we shall do and do it well, that is what I propose and what you shall bring to pass!"

And so the rehearsals went on for weeks, us learning the history and words of "The Marseillaise," about France's glorious ties with America, about her great colonial history in the Americas (with no mention of the slave trade), about the Louisiana Purchase (with no mention of Native Americans pillaged and murdered), and about her great gift to New York Harbor in the wake of the Eiffel Tower. And each day Miss Murphy railed against the barbarian peoples of Algeria and Indochina—how could they not be grateful for the great culture and democracy the French had brought them? How could the people fall dupes to Islamists and Communists? When one of the smarter boys asked how she could hate England for its Irish rule but love France for its colonial power Miss Murphy was quick to recount her own version of Irish history and her sense that had Ireland been a French (and of course Catholic) colony, all would have been fine and dandy.

Meantime, days spread into weeks as us boys sacrificed all our extra time in preparation of the great event and as, hungry for glory, we sang what we called "The Mayonaise" and "Star Speckled Banana" over and over again. And sure enough the great day came, as we all met in the schoolyard for the bus that would take us to New York.

Miss Murphy arrived with a bouquet of flowers she'd undoubtedly bought herself. "Bonjour, boys," she cooed, counting heads and urging the driver, "Allons y!" And when he didn't respond, she shouted, "Let's shove off before it's too late!" We began to laugh and joke, but she brought us up short in no time. "Boys, this is a great opportunity to have a final rehearsal," she said, insisting we sing our songs again and then stand up as she mentioned the names of the Mayor, the French Consul, the other hotshots and of course, France, the United States, New York and New Jersey.

On we sang, up we stood, as the bus jerked and lurched its way out of Elizabeth, passing Newark Airport and making its way finally to the Holland Tunnel. Even there we were forced to sing, and rehearse standing, now in the dark with the roar, din and smoke of the tunnel. Arriving at the docks of New York, we made our way onto the boat sailing to the island. On board, Miss Murphy was unsuccessful in preventing us from mixing with the students from the other two schools there to celebrate this glorious day.

I was not the only boy who found himself drawn to a group of girls dressed in school uniforms who were practicing an acapella version of "Frere Jacques" with a series a trills and tremulous as they sang the round, and then, shockingly, broke into Irving Berlin's musical version of the earnest Emma Lazarus lines, that was one of the few hits from his then new and none-too successful play about the initial gift of Liberty and the hero's search for the statue's original model. But none of this meant anything next to the simple beauty of the girls' singing:

Give me your tired, your poor,
Your huddled masses yearning to breathe free,
The wretched refuse of your teeming shore,
Send these, the homeless, tempest-tost to me,
I lift my lamp beside the golden door!

Seeing and hearing the girls, I felt the wonder of youth and its power to triumph over the likes of Miss Murphy. The sun seemed to shine extra bright and warm, especially as I looked at just one of the girls, who entranced me by her impassioned singing, her girlish knee socks and skirt, and her beautiful round, high cheeked Ashkenazi face framed with the most remarkable long jet-black hair that flowed out over her schoolgirl jacket shoulders and way down her back. Seeing me seeing her with such obvious awe and delight, the girl could not restrain a smile as she continued her song to its end and then jumped in the air in pleasure over the simple, but stirring Berlin melody that expressed the hope of all immigrants and certainly the Jewish immigrants like my own father and all my grandparents, as they came into this same harbor, little realizing that their progeny might end in the hell of Miss Murphy's hot hands, with their only possible redemption being a lovely girl like this one who made lyrics and melody sound more moving and beautiful than anything ever heard before.

"Hi," I said to the girl, approaching her boldly. "It was great and you made it wonderful."

"You could hear me above the other voices?" she said laughing—"That's not good."

"No," I answered, "I didn't hear you alone but I could tell your singing was—beautiful."

"And that's because you think I'm beautiful, right?"

"Yes," was all I managed to say in the face of her boldness, and I knew she was the most alluring girl I'd ever seen or known.

"Well I think you've good taste," she said laughing at me and unbelievably giving me a little peck of a kiss. "My name's Marva," she said laughing again, "as in Marvelous."

"And my name's Mel," I said, "as in Marvelous Marva's melodious new boyfriend," I added, almost rhyming or whatever you call it. And now she just laughed and laughed, brushing her hand against her hair and then wonderfully against my cheek, leaving me utterly speechless until the kids were called to leave the ship and make our way up to the statue, and then climb inside it winding up and up the staircase to the top. Each group was kept apart from the other, with Miss Murphy pushing and shoving to see that her group went first, so that I had no chance to talk to Marva as we climbed. But reaching the crown and peak holes, I lingered until her group arrived and then I stepped aside, saying "Look Marva, look how great Manhattan looks from here," and I stood at her side as the two of us stared at the skyline in awe and trembling, as much for our instant attraction as for the view itself.

But then the teachers egged the students on and we came tumbling down the metal stairs, round and around, down to the base of the statue and on to the lawn, where the banners were now all laid out and we were all led to our seats and the ceremony began with speech after boring speech and with my group absurdly leaping to our feet at the mention of every dignitary, and every theme Miss Murphy had taught us, as if we were Pavlov's dog responding with our doggy salivations. The other school kids giggled as we, Miss Murphy's victims, jumped up and down like so many jacks in the box. The giggles turned into mocking laughter as the names came one after another and us boys could hardly sit down before we had to stand again.

The French representative launched a big speech about the sculpture of Bartholdi, and its placement so near Ellis Island, so that Liberty became a symbol not only of French-U.S. friendship but of the sufferings and contributions of a world of immigrants and migrants in action throughout the world and especially in New

York. Then each of the three chosen French class groups sang their songs. The first group sang a medeley of French folk songs along with "America the Beautiful" in French. Then came Miss Murphy's group with our unimaginative rendition of the Marseillese, with shouts to Armes as if war were ready to break out on the island of Liberty. And then came the girls' group from Queens, singing the French round and then Irving Berlin's song with great conviction and wonderful technique, their voices rising up to the crown of Liberty and even up through the torch-holding arm as if it reached toward heaven.

And in that star-spangled moment of Liberty, I looked at my darling new friend, the flame of my torch in less than a bundle of minutes, and knew that she was Isaac's Rebecca and Jacob's Rachel at the well, and Robert Taylor's Elizabeth Taylor in *Ivanhoe* all rolled into one—that she was and would ever be my heart's greatest desire and that my only possible path to *her* heart was to resist Miss Murphy and refuse to submit again—refuse to stand up again, no matter whose name was called.

And so it happened that I didn't stand up, and then a few of the boys around me joined in, and then even more boys joined me, while Miss Murphy poked at us with her umbrella and still we would not get up, until she all but jabbed me as she spotted my role as rebellious ringleader. But she failed to get any of us to rise no matter how she poked and flailed and pricked and stabbed; and the kids from the other schools began to laugh and jeer and finally applaud, drowning out the voices of the singers and Miss Murphy's continuous shouts for the boys to stand. And then I did in fact stand. I rose and said in my best French, "Vive la Liberté" As the boys and then all the kids shouted, "Vive la Liberté!" And then it was time to get back on the boat and head back to the docks of New York.

As the boat moved away from the island and closer to the Manhattan dock, Marva and I huddled like Lazarus's teeming masses. "I'm so proud of you for what you did. It's terrible to have a teacher like that."

All I could do was smile and yes, tell her how I wanted to see her again. And all she could say was that she lived so far away that she didn't know how we could do it. Perhaps when I was old enough to have a car, she suggested. But we both saw how hard it would be, even as we exchanged addresses and telephone numbers, managing to sneak a kiss goodbye and then make our separate ways back to the busses that awaited us to take us in different directions.

"I'll wait for your letter and call," she said.

"Yes," I said. But then she got on her bus and I took a seat on mine.

"Boys, I have never been so humiliated in all my years of teaching," ranted Miss Murphy. "You'll soon see the consequences of this outrage," she said, until one of the boys in the back shouted, "Murphy why don't you dry up?"

"Why don't you report us to Joe McCarthy," said another.

As for me, the ringleader, I knew she might flunk me and I'd end up at a second rate college with a second rate life ahead of me. But I was happy for the boys' words of praise for me even as I was lost in thought, thinking of the new love in my life, of the girl more lovely than the Lazarus poem, than the Berlin song and than Liberty itself—she who was the very model and soul of liberty, she who I knew even then that I'd probably never see again.

The Boy Who Loved Ellen Feldman

What if the boy in hiding with Anne Frank survived and reinvented himself after the war? ... This [novel by Ellen Feldman] is the story of what might have happened if the boy [had] ... survived to become a man [who] completely denied his persecution in the Holocaust and his identity as a Jew. But [when Anne's diary is published], Peter begins to spiral into flashbacks, paranoia and guilt as he questions who he is and ... [as his] attempts to bury his past cannot prevent it from seeping into his present life. [Excerpts from blurbs and reviews of Ellen Feldman's novel, The Boy Who Loved Anne Frank].

1.

It was somehow just like in her book, it dawned on him, as he sat in a psychiatrist's office unable to speak his mind and wondering how and why this was so. But in his case, he had not repressed the memory of the cause. It was the book that brought it all on, the book which spoke to affinities with the author, the book which reminded him of the books he'd not written, and the life he'd not had as he made his way into the other lives and worlds that were to make him who he was to be.

Of course the book confronted him with her triumph and his relative failure: the girl who with her keen sense of history, had gone her own way out of his vague dreams and troubled life, into the world that would lead her to a penthouse looking down on other, supposedly lesser New Yorkers, perhaps including his Rican relatives, he mused—those still in the barrio and those from the Bronx visiting the relatives who hadn't yet gotten out. But in spite of the vast differences, there were the similarities that made him speechless—his own break with his roots, but his visits to the famous house over the years (had she and he ever visited the same day or month or year?).

Perhaps that similarity was one of several, marking deeper affinities they'd never explored in their short time of connection but he'd felt even if she hadn't. She was the teen queen of his New Jersey life; she was to have been his muse as he wrote his great novelistic opus. He'd loved and lost her all so quickly, and he'd so quickly said goodbye to all that, while she ended up not the muse to any male writer, but the author of several novels, including at least a couple dealing with topics and themes which he himself had hoped to write about—about the Scottsboro case later, but above all this earlier one about Anne Frank's Peter who so many years ago had said that if he survived the Nazis he would come to live his post-Holocaust and not so Jewish life in the very state in which Mel had loved and lost Ellen. Peter had confided in her that if he got out alive, he would reinvent himself entirely. Strangely, though with gigantic differences, it is true, the story of what might have happened if the boy in hiding had survived to become a man was in some ways Mel's story as well.

At first it was just the cover which aroused him—the title of her book, her name, and then her picture on the right flap. But then the cover image began to penetrate him, taking him back to evenings when, like the young man in Fitzgerald's "Winter Dreams," he would come up to her imposing house and knock on the impressive front door, wondering if he should not try the back. Then he remembered his own visits to the unimposing canal house in Amsterdam. And then his growing knowledge of the terrible years came back to him and his own initiation to them as surviving boys his own age told stories about camps so different from the ones he was sent to in the New Jersey hills.

It was in those summer nights that he first felt the magnitude of what had happened. It perplexed him through all his years of schooling as he compared the fate of those around him with relatives and family friends who'd been hunted and caught, imprisoned and gassed after having experienced one unspeakable outrage after another. And meanwhile, the Elizabeth girls played Marjorie Morningstar, got their teeth fixed, their noses bobbed and their breasts enlarged as investments for their ventures into the dating nights. And at the same time, their parents joined country clubs, danced to the new Latino sounds and beats, many of them vacationing in Havana and finally moving to Miami.

Feeling rejected by the richer girls, he'd found himself seeking out one younger but so much more somehow refined than the rest, one whose very imposing home with its high roof, long green lawn and monumental double front door awed him as he approached and told him (though he did not hear at first) *impossible, impossible, impossible*.

2.

After all, their few dates didn't go too far, a patter of conversation (they both read one book after another) a puckish kiss, an embrace, some shared happy moments on the way to one place or another. It was understood there would be no ultimate's and nothing that might truly lead them into temptation. But once he found himself kissing her, holding her, knowing he wanted her all to himself, ready to do anything to be with her—and then she ducked her head down and pulled away and he knew she would not easily be with him and that perhaps nothing would come of his deepening feelings for her.

Miserable, he broke away for a time seeking others— the overwhelming Judy Solmon who made out with him, aroused him and then went off to summer camp (he wrote her the lyrics of love songs, and she would have nothing to do with him when she came back), the sexy, dark one from Hillside, also named Ellen, but so different from the one he loved, the absolutely beautiful but somehow vapid one from Teeneck, and then Belle and Lena from Linden, But none of these forays worked, and it was the little ugly duckling Linda from an area of town more working class than his own shabby lower middle class one—Linda who was known to have given herself to one boy and then another under the Bradley Beach boardwalk, whom he now sought out, brought home when his parents weren't there, took her to the bedroom, removed her top and then caressed her breasts over and over again until his erection rose and he found wanting her pearshaped body, just so (as he told himself) he could bear waiting for Ellen.

One day in his house Linda helped him take off her blouse and bra so he could both play with her breasts, cup them, suck them, until their breathing began to roar and she got out of bed and had him bring her an ironing board to unwrinkle her blouse. "I have to go home," she said.

Then one spring evening at her house, her parents on the front porch, they went to her room where he fondled her again and found himself pressing his lips to the outside of her shorts. Funny little girl still in braces, so eager to be touched, willing to risk all for some wonderful caresses. A girl seemingly willing to risk having a reputation, even.

But he could not help but tell his friends as if to declare his independence from Ellen, but the word got around to Linda, and when he met her outside a drugstore after school, she confronted him.

"You told!" she screamed, "You told everyone! Don't come near him again!"

And she left him standing on the corner, and that was that for some years.

That was that for Ellen too, he soon understood. So when he tried to go back to her, she just couldn't seem to find an evening free. And then one day, he saw her walking around with a Princeton scarf with her new older Princeton boyfriend, and that was that. Years later a girl he'd dated briefly, now a grandmother and married for years to one of his better high school friends told him, "I remember you with us on a bus ride, opening your wallet and looking at a photo of Ellen and crying." This was also the friend who told him that Ellen'd become a novelist, and that she'd just written a novel introduced by Arthur Schlessinger, Jr.

He waited some months, as long as he could when he found her book on a fiction shelf under F and there, sure enough, was *Lucy*. And there too was a photo of Ellen, now in her sixties, looking (when could the photo have been taken?) just like the girl who'd left him, and, yes, just like the girl in the photo snapshot he'd cried over some forty-five years before.

3.

Ellen's rejection led him to step up his school activities, become a school vice president, then president, try out for football, be a leader in the school glee club and end up chosen to sing in the statewide double quartet. He joined the campus newspaper as special editor, joined the school debate team, and helped raise its level. All his energies went out, he withdrew from his more intellectual friends, even trying to water down the things he wrote, until he was less distinguishable from the other teens.

And still the dark sides of his personality kept coming forth, as he kept searching for some special love such as he had felt and still felt for Ellen as he continued to write stories and plays without much inspiration or flair but with always the danger of a turn toward the morbid and depressing.

Meanwhile, he and many of his friends were so rejected by the Jewish girls of his own age and even younger, that they began to fan out, expanding the range of their search out toward the Oranges, up to Teaneck or down to New Brunswick—and even over to Brooklyn where they were stopped cold by Syrian Jewish gangs who wore their mezuzahs the way Italians and Latinos wore their crosses, carried switchblades and let the Elizabeth boys know that they didn't quite appreciate the invasion of their turf and the dogging of "their women."

At Dartmouth, he would find no love. In Berkeley, there would be Sylvia, who also left him, leaving him broken, playing Sinatra torch songs in his small dark room, only gradually recovering, to make new friends, but then falling again for Laura Rachel, beautiful Saint Lawrence girl, so talented and true: Rachel, on leave from the college and boyfriend, who introduced him to Bartok quartets and bedded with him once claiming thereafter that she'd made a mistake—that she still loved and would now be true to David…

And that was that—the store closed. He so racked and embittered by this loss, he was never to date a Jewish girl again for many years, though when he met Marlena, he thought she was Jewish or Mexican, only to find, already deeply drawn to her, that she was an Italian American woman only deeply drawn to women. Though that or her infidelities male and female didn't stop him from living with her for two plus years and marrying her for another two plus.

And that was just the beginning of the trail he had blazed west that then shifted toward Mexico, Central America and beyond, as he lived his life as a non-Jewish Jew, denying his identity somewhat as Ellen's Peter would deny his, marrying not a Jewish woman as did Peter (and as did many non-Jews) but marrying an Italian American who looked Jewish, a Nicaraguan who didn't and then a relative maybe of one of those Puerto Ricans Ellen stared down on from the penthouse she shared with her psychiatrist husband, she having found the fountain of youth and not aging in all those years (a regular Dorian Grey was she), while he grew older and older as the years rolled by—until that one day when, somehow, he discovered her Anne Frank book and saw in it all those Philip-Rothian reflections on his own fate with her, the experience filling him with memories but leaving him speechless in the office of a psychiatrist (he hoped it was not Ellen's husband) as he tried to figure out the whys and wherefores of it all.

4.

He had first visited Ann Frank's house with Marlena in the fall of 1964. They had been in Paris some weeks, and then on they went to the tawdry city with prostitutes in the windows, with Rembrandt, Hals, Vermeer and Van Gogh, with the old Jewish district, the Concertgebow Orchestra Hall and all the jazz you could want with your Bols gin at Leidzaplein. But now it was time for the house, the entrance, as they saw the group of somber German schoolkids obligated by law to visit in groups, to feel guilty and remember what they had never directly experienced going through the map-blocked entrance and into the space where the Jewish families lived hidden all those months.

Immediately he, like Ellen before or after him, experienced the dank air, the claustrophobia of the place. Immediately the whole experience of the Holocaust became concentrated in this little space and in the diary written here entry by entry as the war went on. He suddenly remembered the survivor stories in summer camp, the films he'd seen, and yes, the day when his usually supercilious Berkeley professor, an astute analyst of Yeats and Elliot who had recently defended *Howl* in court, informed his students that he had just read *Reflections in a Golden Eye* and come to the conclusion that *The Diary of a Young Girl* was more important than the contrived subjective horrors of Carson McCullers, Flannery O'Conner and other southern-gothic writers of our day.

Now in the room itself, the space he'd imagined from the book and then seen in play and film, he felt overwhelmed by history, by the real pains of others and the failure of his own feeble efforts to create fictions truer and more expressive of life and history. At that time, he knew nothing of the censorship Otto Frank had exerted on the diary; nor did he know of the falsifications which the playwrights and film writers had added to adorn or supposedly deepen the drama. Only through Ellen's book would he know how the story of Peter's stolen bread was a manipulation by playwrights seeking to satisfy audience wishes for drama; only through her book did he see Peter rise and protest the falsification of his father's life and character and did he experience the wish to do the same when he took his Puerto Rican daughter and grandson to see *The Diary* in a revised version incorporating some of Frank's cuts but maintaining the fundamental falsification concocted by the original playwrights.

He would leave the Frank house room to see the downstairs exhibit of the Holocaust and wonder about the guilt trip laid on the German kids—what must they have thought about their complicity or their parents? Then he left, only to return on a trip some years later with his Nicaraguan wife, and then again after a conference on Chicano literature, when he more or less led a group of key writers and professors through the house and, on leaving, more or less led them to a plaque which cites Otto Frank dedicating the efforts of his foundation to the prevention of further attacks not only on Jews, but on any people. He was so relieved to see this message, so proud to share it with his Chicano friends, themselves victims of discrimination, sometimes, he knew (and they were quick to remind him) from Jews.

Finally, years later, as he made plans to visit the house with Esther, his third and last wife (she from Puerto Rico), Harriet, a Dutch-Jewish Holocaust survivor friend asked why they were making so much of Anne Frank, when there were many other girls like Harriet herself who had been among those hidden by Christian families in the countryside, and whose stories were perhaps as compelling as ones that were better known. And then, he explained that it was because it was Anne Frank and not the survivors who had written the diary from whence had come the play and film, and also, he added, that Anne Frank had died in the Holocaust while she, Harriet, like many of the other girls so successfully hidden, had not.

So he took his Esther, who had read the book but now felt the full impact of taking the walk. It was fine to be there with her and sense her gravitas, and then meet Harriet and her husband, a fellow Jewish-American of Mel's own age who had lived his own version of Jewish-American life in the New York-New Jersey area, and to be taken by them on a tour of Amsterdam's Jewish sector, with its memorials to pre-Holocaust Jewish life and the Holocaust itself.

But through all this, they both only knew the full effect of their visit by relating it to a prior tour they had taken of Auschwitz some days after visiting Warsaw and Krakow. Arriving on a rainy day, they spent hours with an Argentine Jewish friend slogging through rain and mud, depressed and overwhelmed by all they saw.

He came upon the photo of a victim who bore the same last name as a wing of his family. But perhaps even more impressive to them both was seeing the display of battered suitcases and among them, one labelled "Maria Kafka." The writer of *The Trial* had died of tuberculosis in 1924. And look where he might well have ended had he lived so long. Of course, the writer's two sisters had lived on, only, like Anne herself, to die before World War II came to an end. Was this the suitcase of one of the sisters? And did that really matter? What story could one create from this possibility, another what-if story that as good as was Ellen Feldman's book could not begin to represent the horror and the proof of a godless universe that was so evident and palpable in this day at Auschwitz.

His wife immediately related the horrors of Auschwitz to the worse things that had happened to Puerto Ricans under the Spanish and then the U.S. She thought immediately of her brother, like so many other Puerto Ricans, sent to Viet Nam to pay their horrendous dues for all the wonderful things they had won through the honor of their colonization and citizenship. Meanwhile, Mel and his Argentine Jewish friend remained silent as they went to dinner in Crakow, ordering filet mignon and a fine wine to give thanks and yes laugh and celebrate even as they cried for having lived through the painful day, and for not having suffered and died in the Holocaust.

None of these encounters and speculations produced a novel such as Ellen Feldman was able to write. No matter what capacity for writing fiction he once might have had, he could find no inspiration as she found from her own visits. It was not the first time he'd had to recognize the limits of his imagination. Once he read a wonderful poem about going up an elevator he himself had gone up for some twenty-two years in his job, and realized that he never had thought of writing a poem about that elevator ride. So too he had never written about his Anne Frank encounters although just a few months before Ellen published her novel he had attended a conference on Central America and been highly criticized by an older Jewish Latin Americanist for having labelled the slaughter of indigenous people in the mountains of Guatemala as a "holocaust"—a word that should only designate one horrendous experience.

Thinking of this attack he had written the following lines in an essay on Rigoberta Menchú:

A half century plus of broken utopian dreams, holocaust, and attempts to deny holocaust.... And I have centered my life work not on the experience of the group into which I was born, but rather on the horrors and traumas faced by other human collectivities in other, often very different historical conjunctures. ... Maybe it was when he heard a story of Palestinian displacement, so much like the displacements he had heard of before, but now with the kind of role reversals that have haunted people like Noam Chomsky. Maybe that's where his journey began, or maybe it was those photos from Auschwitz, or maybe it was staring at the images of Orozco at Dartmouth's Baker library images calling, testifying until he went off to California, and some years later, started heading south. ...

Where not these words pretty much his life and writerly credo? What combination of imagination and discipline, talent and dedication led to the production of deep narrative? Did he have the capacity? He felt he'd had it, hadn't used it and now it might well be out of his reach. And why was that? What had happened to him? All he knew was that she who he'd imagined as his muse had gone on her own way, while he on the other hand had spent years going one way and then another without any constant trajectory.

Of course the drift came with failed love. And so with Ellen's rejection the seeds were planted that led to his first wife, Marlena—and indeed beyond her, to his second wife and the Latin American women who were to follow him after those first encounters. Meanwhile he'd gone off to get B.A. and M.A. and then after six years of teaching and travel, and countless years after leaving New Jersey and Ellen behind, starting in a Comparative Literature Ph.D. program. And meanwhile she went off to some fine school, got her early degree, and then he MA and Ph.D. in history, before drawing on her historical turn to write some failed novels but finally writing her breakthrough text, *Lucy*.

And then one day he saw the book, looked her up in google and found a link leading him to an interview with the author, and hearing for the first time in more than fifty years her voice so like the voice he could barely remember discussing oh-so-coherently and well the effects of repressed memory and identity flight in the case of Peter Van Dan.

To think she too was so connected with a Jewish past she'd left behind in the wave of U.S. life from the fifties on, to hear that voice that he'd thought was to bring him joy in his life as he wrote his great plays and novels... She who had written several good books, been praised in *The New York Times*, gone on to write of the Scottsboro boys, of World War II wives and other things, as she, like he, raced to her life's end producing book after book, knowing all too well that she could never produce a book as important as *The Diary of a Young Girl*, but doing what she could as well as she could until there was no could left.

And who was he as he floated through his declining years, a Latin Americanist distanced from Anne Frank, New Jersey and New York, distanced from the world of post-Holocaust Jewry, as he lived his very different life. How had he managed his world in New Jersey and then after? What had happened to his child religiosity? His Jewish heart's lonely hunting?

Perhaps he could not write any novels, but yes, he could write stories, little vignettes, mini- and maxi semi-fictions that, taken together, were for better or worse the novels making the novel of his life. ... And yes he wished Ellen Feldman well as if she needed his good wishes, hoped she fell to no painful or otherwise terrible disease and hoped she would never have to read his work, that it was better at this stage of things for each of them to do what they needed to do and leave it at that.

The Italian Americans
(1956-57)

1.

The first Italian Americans Mel knew were the kids he met on the streets playing football, and even throughout the apartment complex his family moved to in his teens. The Italians and Blacks fought every day in the schoolyard while the Jews stayed clear, stood on the sidelines and prepped for their parents' dream of college. As one of two Jewish football players on the freshman high school roster, he garnered Black and Italian votes (the Jewish ones he had wrapped up from the git-go) and won the elections for school president. He got to know one of the most decent and sweetest of the Italian kids, Carmine, and they became good friends, doing homework together sometimes at school or even at Carmine's house, going sometimes together to explore Manhattan or other New York worlds.

Carmine was the only Italian who was voted on the first go-round into the Sabres—a club and not a gang, they were quick to underline. Carmine's older sister was a senior doing her last year as football cheerleader. Mel would see her sometimes at Carmine's house and developed a crush as he watched her do her turns, her skirt flying and he caught a glimpse of panties, a gift from the cruel November wind.

But, as he found out years later, a spunky girl named Georgina had targeted him for flirting in the new apartment complex, apparently her first Jewish adventure, as she and then another Italian girlfriend visited his apartment while his parents were at work, and the girls teased him to the limits as he chased them around the living room into the bedroom, giggling and running, letting him kiss them once in awhile, stirring his imaginings to madness.

Then one day, Georgina's brother, one of his Italian football buddies said to him, "Look, you're ok, you know, but don't go messing with my sister."

"Well tell her not to come over," he said without much gaallantry.

"You bet I will," said the brother, "But if she does come there, you keep her out, or your ass is grass."

Georgina never came over again, but her girlfriends did, knocking on his door and not taking no for an answer until one of them finally admitted that Georgina would get the full reports and wanted to know if anything happened. Mel tried to oblige, but the girl went running from the apartment.

2.

Then came another day when still another girl came by, just the most beautiful and amazing sweetheart Mel had ever seen, more tempting maybe than any one Mel had ever known before—with skin more olive than Carmine's sister, with hair darker and cut pixie-short, and her breasts peering out from her blouse, her pretty thighs peeking out from her plaid mini-skirt, her face and eyes a total knockout.

"Hi," she said, "I'm Maxine Lambrini and I live two buildings over. I'm one of the Italian girls. Can I come in? Mel just stood dumbfounded and finally let her in.

"Maxine doesn't sound too Italian," he said.

"It's not," she said. "My mom's Jewish and my dad's Sicilian," she told him.

Mel was amazed, he didn't even know that such pairings were possible and, it appeared, quite legal. But he certainly liked the results and suddenly the door of life opened and he felt it was he who entered the apartment, which was now some kind of heaven.

She walked around the family digs rather gingerly at first, checking out the scene—going straight to the menorah in the dining room cupboard and looking at it with a certain awe.

"We have a menorah too," she said. "But my mom hasn't taught me about it."

"Where do you go to shul?" he asked, "I've never seen you before."

"I don't go to shul and I don't go to any of that silly stuff. I don't have Jewish girlfriends or boyfriends, except maybe you!" she laughed and then she shocked Mel by giving him a kiss right on the mouth.

"But I won't go with you if you're one of those complete mama boy yids—my mom couldn't stand them and neither can I—with their funny little caps and whiskers, and their black suits and smelly bodies!"

"I'm not like those kids," Mel said, trying to meet her standards. "I don't even believe in God," he said, "and I'm not raising money for Israel," he said putting all his qualifications on the table. "And you can see my mom's not around—I'm a latchkey kid so you can come around almost any day and find me just by myself."

"That sounds like fun," she said, putting her hand on his knee and kissing him again. "And that's just what I heard."

"What do you mean?"

"I mean all the Italian girls here say you're a sweetheart, but that I'm the perfect one for you, cause you're not as Jewish as the other Jewish boys, and you like Italian girls at least as much as Jewish ones. So we were made for each other."

"I don't know," Mel said, suddenly turning bold. "I'm not so sure we're such a perfect fit," he said, staring her in the eye, then, moving his mouth ever so close to hers, and finally giving her a full mouth and tongue kiss which she returned with the sweetest excitement.

"Not bad," she said, laughing, and then sighing as if imagining a more total encounter. "See you sometime soon," she said, and with that she gave him one peck on the cheek and ran out the door.

3.

Mel waited for what seemed forever for Maxine to come to see him again. For a whole week she had him waiting, with his every idle thought turning to her and all she promised to bring his life. He tried to ply his books, tried to party with his friends. But Maxine was ever on his mind, and he didn't know how to make her visit come to pass.

Sure enough, one day, sitting alone at home, he heard a knock on the door and there she was, dressed like a schoolgirl her short-cropped hair making her look almost boyish in the sexiest female way.

"Can I come in?" she asked. And all he could do was open the door wider and let her pass underneath his arm. She looked around the apartment once again, and then she went right to the living room couch.

"Sit down with me," she said, and, speechless he did what she said.

"Look," she said, "I know you were crazy waiting for me to come over."

"How do you know?" he said trying to act defiant.

"Don't let's play games, Mel," she said. "I know you're all hot for me. You're crazy about me and I'm kinda crazy about you. I may even be in love with you," she said. "But I'm not gonna get pregnant in high school. I'm not sure I'm going to college but I know you are. I even know who you've been in love with and I know she dropped you like a hot potato for a college boy, so you're sure to go to college now—just to show her you're as good as her boyfriend. And where will that leave us?"

Mel was shocked by her detective work and powers of deduction. He wondered how she knew about his true love Ellen and the hell he was in from losing her—even though, to be sure, he had never had her except in his mind. In a way he was scandalized by Maxine's snooping, but happy that she cared.

"Besides," she said, "if my father ever found out we were here alone or maybe doing things, he'd probably kill us both. But you for sure."

Mel had no reason to doubt her words. He had done some snooping of his own and had found that her father was some kind of petty Mafioso who could prove dangerous if he found out that his precious princess daughter was messing around with a nogoodnik Russian Jewish on his father's side and (lowest of the low) Romanian Jewish on his mother's. Mel knew Maxine knew the score, but neither she nor he could control their emotions. She just had to come close to him and their bodies would spring into action.

She came over with her homework and before you know it, they were kissing. They would catch each other's air and sigh and before you knew it, he was stroking her sweet breasts, and she was breathing hard against his erection. Soon her blouse would be off and they were lying on the bed, fearful to complete their passion, she shifting gears and talking about their love and early marriage, he feeding her fantasies as he touched her everywhere and got her to touch him. Once in while they'd go to a movie together in his beat-up green '52 Chevy, but before you knew it, they weren't watching the movie but kissing and sighing and stroking until neighboring viewers would tell them to stop it or get out. One crazy night, the manager shined the flashlight on them and all but pushed them out the door.

They came back to the complex, but his parents might be home and he couldn't ask her up, so that, deep into their passion, they got in the back seat of his car and picked up where they'd left off in the theater, when suddenly there was another glare on them, but this time it was her father who shined his flashlight, and then yanked open the car door, and then pulled Mel from the car.

"You think you got it pretty good here!" He screamed. "You think you can mess around with my daughter and get away with it."

"Daddy," Maxine cried.

"You go up upstairs!" he shouted. "Your putana days are over… And you, my fine Jewish boy, don't ever let me see you with her again, or you'll have a second circumcision and wish you never messed with the likes of us. We don't go for fucking around, you understand."

"But—"

"Do you understand?"

"Yessir," he responded, and then went to his apartment.

A few days later, he called her, but she said she couldn't talk. Day after day, he tried to find her after school. But he never found her. He tried calling her again and again, and finally got her.

"Maxine," he pleaded. "I want to see you."

"You can't, we can't see each other anymore."

"Not even after school? —I've waited for you every day hoping we could talk."

"We can't talk," she said, "and don't wait for me after school cause I don't go there anymore. My dad transferred me to a Catholic school, and my mother's too scared to say a word."

"But you're half-Jewish, Maxine."

"Not anymore," she said.

And when he tried to say more, to tell her how perfect she was, how he wanted her to be with him through college and then through his entire life—she his Hebrew Juliet not from Verona but further south, she just said, "That's what we thought, but that can never be. My father's not Italian, he's Sicilian and that's worse. And when he says no, it's no."

4.

Mel mourned and moped for some days, but his young high school life rolled on. In the summer, his father prevailed on one of the high-placed Italian union leaders who came to his restaurant and played high stakes gin rummy with him to get his son a high paying job as a construction worker. Pretty soon he was an apprentice hod carrier, preparing steel beams with oil, dumping and mixing cement and carting wheel barrels full of cinder blocks as he eagerly went about his tasks. Sometimes he went too fast, and one of the Italian workers, Gino, would say, "Hey kid, take it easy, don't kill the job!"

Soon he joined the workers in playing cards and smoking, while they mounted up their hourly pay and went for time and a half overtime—and a good time was had even by Mel who had learned to play the game as it should be played.

Mel sometimes thought of Maxine, but he worked long hours, while a newfound fascination with jazz often sent him out of town to Greenwich Village, and his frequent race track nights with his father sent them roaring past Manhattan to the trotters at Yonkers Raceway or even further out across the Triborough Bridge to Roosevelt Raceway on Long Island, his dad letting him listen to jazz coming and going, and them picking horses and often winning, as his kiddy for college grew.

During the summer Mel's cousin-enemy Howard ended his lifetime gastronomic virginity by introducing his kosher-bound but now wandering palate to the vomit-smelling joys of pizza. Soon after, he and his friends abandoned his dad's restaurant, and, with Carmine as leader, they'd go once every so often to a house that had been converted into an Italian restaurant where they'd share a pizza and individual plates with spaghetti and veal parmigiana. When the owners realized that Mel was the son of a would-be semi-swanky Jewish (but not so Kosher) restaurateur from another part of town, they were both impressed and wary, asking him if his parents weren't unhappy with his not eating there and bringing his friends to their restaurant.

"No," he responded, "they understand we love Italian food"; and one day he surprised them by bringing by his dad, who, irreverent Jew that he was, ordered a pasta with sausage and gulped it down with great pleasure.

"This is great food," he told him. "I wish my chef could make a few Italian plates this rich." And the couple was so pleased and blessed, and Mel so proud that he almost forgot Maxine.

But it really wasn't so easy, because that very summer, his aunt announced that her darling son Leonard was marrying a beautiful Italian girl, Pat. Mel went to the wedding and socialized with all the Italians present, hoping that Maxine and even her dad might be there, and all the time wondering why Pat and Leonard couldn't be Maxine and him. And it would've made it a lot easier her being half Jewish and therefore his children Jewish after all, he thought. And he wondered how his father could play cards with Italian and maybe Sicilian gangsters and incur dangerous debts with the likes of the horrendous Sicilian father who had destroyed his perfect Jewish-Italian love.

A couple of times in the next few months, Mel's father disappeared from sight and when he asked where he was, his mother would say he was in the Turkish baths, when the truth was, as Mel well knew, that he was in hiding, looking for money to pay back one or more of his Italian friends to prevent one or more of them from breaking his legs and more. Somehow, he always found the cash and was free to appear again, take out Mel again, though no matter how many times Mel asked, he never said anything against the Italians and the roles so many of them played in his life.

5.

But perhaps the biggest of all these Italian moments of his youth was toward the end of his last year of high school, when, Mario Fulani, an Italian neighbor of his father's restaurant claimed that the place was rat-infested and urged that the restaurant be closed down. Fulani began to organize some of the Italians in the neighborhood against the restaurant, and at one point, Mel's father made an appointment with Carmine's father. Mr. Liotta, a very respected, Church-going accountant, was very friendly and said he'd do what he could to calm the neighbors—but of course only if my father swore there were no rats, which of course he did.

But, as Mel's father told him, when Mr. Liotta sought to defend him and tried to settle things without litigation, Fulani could not be appeased and even accused Carmine's father of selling out to the Jews. Then, as if to protect himself against any aspersions, Fulani went and got himself a Jewish lawyer, insisted on his day in court, and got it. As that day approached, Mel went with his father to consult once more with Mr. Liotta, who, with Carmine at his side, suggested that that there was something fishy about this case, that whoever was behind it was not the man who seemed to be leading the band and that the only way out of this mess would be to somehow discredit his accuser. Mr. Liotta offered no more insight into the matter, but he suggested that, in view of Fulani's choice in lawyers, Mel's father should get himself an Italian lawyer to help with the case.

The next day, Carmine called Mel and told him he'd learned that Fulani or whoever was helping him might have hired someone to plant and photograph rats on the restaurant parking lot. And now, the more he thought about it, the more Mel came to believe that he and his aborted love affair with Maxine were the cause of all this trouble. He wasn't sure, but it did occur to him that the rat behind the rats was her revengeful father; and it occurred to him as well, that the only solution to the problem was for him to go after the photo-taker and take some photos of his own.

Of course it was terribly risky. What if the one planting the rats was a hired professional, and what if the pro got wind of him— an amateur photographer at best? What if he got cornered and caught? But on the other hand, he thought, he was the apparent cause of his father's problems and if he didn't come forward to help him, who would? So, unbeknownst to his father, Mel knew what his new Italian job (his last high school job and his true graduation) was going to be: to spy for his father and save the business he'd worked so hard to build.

Right away, he called Carmine and asked if he would join him—if he would go with him as his driver and fellow spy, and maybe, just by being Italian himself, protect him some if things went bad. "Sure I'll help," said Carmine, "first because you're my friend and then because like my father says, there's no one we should hate more than an Italian who gives us all a bad name."

Carmine went with Mel to the camera store and helped him choose the best, high-powered camera good for shooting in the dark. Then, that night, the two young men waited in Mel's green Chevy in a secluded part of the restaurant parking lot, in between a few cars and trucks that always parked there.

Mel had the camera all set, but nothing happened for hours, and the two were almost worn out from the waiting and worrying, when a figure who looked not like a pro, but Fulani himself, appeared with a bag and emptied out what might well be some king-size rats into the rear area of the restaurant. Mel snapped photos of the figure approaching the rear area bag in hand, of his letting the rats spring from the bag onto the ground, and then, of his photographing the rats around the garbage bin.

"Looks like you got it!" Carmine said with some glee, revving up the motor and racing his car out of the parking lot, he and Mel laughing all the way home.

6.

The next day, Mel delivered the photos to his father's lawyer; and just a few days later, the hearing took place. Mel went with his father to the court, saw Fulani with some friends and apparent supporters, but then he spotted some more friendly faces in the small crowd—Carmine and his father, the husband and wife from the Italian restaurant, some of his Italian football teammates, and even some of his construction worker pals, who signaled to him from their seats. On went the proceedings with the neighbor's slick-haired lawyer helping him paint the darkest, most terrible picture of the restaurant, and then show a series of photos of the rats around the restaurant garbage bin. Then it was the turn of Mel's father's lawyer, who, instead of calling on Mel's father, immediately called on Mel to testify. Nervous as he was, Mel looked out hoping to see Maxine, but she wasn't there.

"Are these your photos?" asked the lawyer.

"Yes," said Mel, explaining how he shot the photo of the rats being placed and photographed on the parking lot, and how an Italian—no, Sicilian—friend, present in court, was witness to the whole thing.

The judge looked over Mel's photos and then asked the two lawyers to step up, conferring with one, then another and then both. He then stated softly that he would entertain a petition to dismiss the case; and the lawyers concurred.

Unable to believe his lawyer's words of agreement, Fulani leaped from his seat. "Dirty Jewish tricks!" he screamed. And it was then that the judge remonstrated against the neighbor's fraud that could still send him to jail. "My lawyer isn't defending me. You are accusing me without any real evidence. I didn't plant any rats! Somebody has sold me out!" he screamed.

"Mr. Fulani, for your own good, I will hold you in contempt of court if you persist," warned the judge, slamming down his gavel, "Case dismissed."

Mel's father seemed dazed, as Carmine's family came up to him with words of congratulations. Mel gave Carmine a big hug, and his sister gave him a kiss on the cheek "I know you like me," she whispered.

"Yes," he said under his breath, "But it was never to be."

And in the midst of it all, it occurred to him that maybe Mr. Liotta himself, or one of his less reputable friends or relatives, had actually planted and photographed the rats that night. And it even dawned on him that maybe it wasn't Fulani who had planted the rats after all; and that maybe (horror of horrors), his father's restaurant was in fact infested with rats.

But now, amidst the handshakes and hugs, the slaps on his back, the congrats to his father and even the praise heaped on Mel ("That's a fine son you got there," "That boy's got a future," "You should be proud")—even with all this, Mel kept his eyes roaming about the courtroom above all to see if Maxine just might be there.

And there, toward the back of the courtroom, he saw not her, but her father, Mr. Lambrini, who, glaring and glowering, just stared at Mel as if he was the only one there.

And all the time, Mel kept thinking of his daughter—the beautiful girl he had not seen for weeks and months and whom he was never to ever see again.

The African Americans

1. My Mother and Her Atavisms

When my mother's mother died and her father married again, the story goes, she was so unhappy with her cold stepmother and so lonely that she didn't know what to do. Her brothers teased her about her normal childhood fear of cats and dogs, making it worse and indeed a near lifetime aversion she could not control. The fear of cats was so great that she one night left a favorite New York Jewish dairy restaurant Ratners 1, because a cat appeared; and she refused to enter a nearby Ratners 2, because she apparently thought that cats came with the chain.

"Besides," she told us, already frustrated from being excluded from the wellknown eatery we'd hoped to eat in, "where there's cats, there's rats and that all there is to that, especially at Ratners."

And of course she wouldn't even think of going to the most famous deli in the old neighborhood, if only because its name began with K but sounded like the plural of cat, and at the same time rhymed with the rodent the cats most like to catch. Obviously, the fear of the other had entered her life very early on.

All this to place in context what I'm about to recount, and also delay, I admit, telling of things that were uncomfortable to me and helped me keep my distance from some of the other Jews I knew in our New Jersey world and my life thereafter. I mean there's no question I've almost always had Jewish friends in my life out of affinity and affect. But it's also true they've almost all been non-Jewish Jews like me. One reason being the materialist strain of American Jewry, the synagogue-centered life I early rejected, the ever more right wing leanings of many fellow Jews, including many in my family who I loved as kids and still found a kind of kinship with but couldn't tolerate for the chauvinist and Zionist attitudes they espoused, and yes their attitude toward many "others," whether cats, dogs, goyim or Blacks.

Anyway, so the story goes, my mother saw that a Black woman down the street from her father's house always lined up her kids at the place where they waited each day for the school bus; and when she saw that bus approaching, she went down the row tidying up and kissing each kid with great warmth and affection. And sure enough, it became my mother's way to come down to that same place and wait on the same line to get that Black woman's kiss and blessing before she followed that woman's Black kids on the bus.

I guess there is something touching to me in all this, though I sometimes regret feeling that the story's been told to me to show just how desperate my mother must have been not just for seeking love from another, but from a Black mother at that. Somehow the story doesn't confirm for me my mother's transcendence of racism but rather her desperate search for love despite what some consider as "a natural aversion"—and by a girl afraid of cats and rats if not her own shadow.

2. Jews and the Others

To be sure, the Jews were often averse to all others—they were all goyim—people who drank too much, fucked too much and ate trashy food not fit for better people. They were also often uneducated and coarse, having frequently followed a false God, or a false messiah who led them down the garbage-filled road they followed. Of course there were all the anti-semite scum and then there were all the others—the followers of Mohamed on the one hand, and the descendants of Ham on the other. And the only people who might be lower and worse than these were those Jews who left their own people behind—those who mixed, lived among, shared thoughts and passions and worst of all, married or otherwise, fucked with goyim or Blacks on a regular basis. Surely an occasional encounter could occur from passions pent up due to the success of Jewish parents in keeping their daughters virgins—at least so went that story too; and while it wasn't right, it was certainly minimally understandable that little Moisha might stick his pen in the wrong inkwell.

In my mother's case, things must have become worse, as her Romanian Jewish family moved from East Orange down to Newark where great numbers of Blacks and Jews began to fill the city until the Jews began to move out of town to all the surrounding towns and townships, leaving the Blacks behind, or so they thought.

Maybe it was true that many Jews had been involved in the slave trade in the Spanish as well as the Dutch and other Caribbeans. Maybe it was true that there were more than one or two Shylock types lurking about. But at least some of the Jews of my generation were heirs to the Jewish Enlightenment, rebels against the narrow mentalities of their parents who generalized the "Never Again" of post-Holocaust talk to mean what it did on the great placard at the Anne Frank House which said in effect: "Never let this happen again to Jews or any other people." As Holocaust survivors even if raised in the relative safety of the U.S. as they found it, this sector of American Jewery would have nothing to do with Jewish racism and exploitation and would seek to apply what they considered the best of the Jewish tradition in their own secular lives.

Many of the kids of those families who escaped anti-Jewish pograms and programs and came to this country (those huddled masses yearning to be free) were the teachers, social workers, lawyers and doctors of the Blacks in their community; and, at least so it was said, many of them fought as radicals, liberals or maybe just do-gooders against racist prejudice, discrimination and exploitation. It is to the absolute credit of many of these sons and daughters that no matter what racist attitudes might have affected them, a great number of them were willing to risk their lives in Civil Rights campaigns, marches and demonstrations until they retreated as Black Nationalism and Muslim politics spread throughout the urban centers and fiery speakers spoke out against patronizing and bloodsucking, Jews who as employers and landlords exploited Blacks and Latinos to the max.

3. My Mother and Virginia

Of course, my father was indeed a Jewish boss, who hired an older Negro named Carl, to work with him on catering affairs. But, I always believed that he was just the opposite of the exploiting Jew who felt it was part of his duty in this world to rise above the ghettoism of Jewish life even if he remained and never ceased to be at once a progressive Jew but also a Zionist. No, my father's failings were tied up with other things, but not the Jewish-Black question. Or at least so it seemed to me at the time.

However, my mother's world was very different from my father's since she was only a boss at home; and her world was nothing like the next generation of Jewish freedom fighters either. The reality of her life could not be measured by business decisions or by great causes and concerns but by her relationship with the household and yes with the housemaid she eventually hired to do the housework once a week.

Virginia by first name (I don't think we ever knew the last) was a small and humble woman recently up from the south, with a gentle smile featuring a big gold tooth and a good sense of humor who seemed to do all my mother asked, and who won my mother's begrudging affection but who nevertheless was ever the Black servant so different from ourselves.

The worst of her relationship with Virginia was that my mother kept a separate plate, cup, glass and silverware for her Black maid. "They're just not kosher," she explained to me.

I sensed her fear of contamination, from an unkosher body, maybe a fear of Blackness and Black blood somewhat similar to her fear of cats and dogs. Indeed a culminating moment of my childhood and my struggle with my own people was the day when, no one at home, I went to the kitchen, took down Virginia's drinking glass, filled it with milk, mixed in some chocolate and swallowed it in spite of the cringing fear and aversion I had somehow learned to feel even as I was conquering it with this action.

Also out of rebellion, I left the glass in the sink for my mother to find. "Mel," she asked, "Did you drink out of Virginia's glass? I told you that her utensils were strictly for her, and she would be very upset if she knew you had been disrespecting her things."

So, my blasphemy was kept a secret from Virginia and the whole world, except for my mother and me. And she was a pretty good keeper of every one's secrets, though I, as you can see in this story, was and am not.

It should be said finally that my mother was a woman who became better as she grew older. In early old age, she learned to love her daughter's little dogs as long as they kept some distance. She was good enough to accept my first difficult, Italian wife, my second Nicaraguan wife and son, and my third Puerto Rican wife, even though, light-skinned as she was, she might well have African blood as part of her genes. It seemed to me that, especially after my father died, my mother dedicated her final years of life to loving all. And I always took the opportunity to introduce her to my Black friends and to take her to see and thoroughly enjoy Billy Daniels or Joe Williams or whoever, especially when they played in distinguished venues like Carnegie Hall or Chicago's Orchestra Hall.

4. Other Black Encounters

Before I left New Jersey, I learned to hate Jewish anti-black feelings, actions and discourse.

"Look at that ugly schwarza," said the young man who would marry the daughter of my mother's brother. "Schwarza this and schwarza that" was almost all he could say.

Then there were the attitudes of my Jewish classmates, especially when Rabbi Golub told us of Noah's Black son, and then of Abraham's. And where did these offspring come from? I asked. Weren't we a pure race who only love our own? And yet why was it that even though we were pure, Jews from Russia tended to be blonde and Jews from Africa tended to be Black? I had studied evolution—and I was all for Darwin and not for Lamarck.

One of the greatest scandals that ever broke out in my family was after I left the east coast, and my cousin Bernie discovered his Jewish wife Maxine was having an affair with a Black gym teacher at the school where she taught. Bernie's mother, Ellie, my father's only sister, was always considered the most ladylike and wonderful of ladies who got along so well with her Italian in-laws. But Ellie lost it when she saw her dear boy victimized by a woman she could only refer to as a Jewish whore who'd chosen a Black man over her beloved, wonderful and circumcised son.

To be brief, Bernie divorced and drifted, only to refind and remarry Maxine a few years later. The couple fought through their problems but the mother who had spoken out too much, saying too much that was ugly, could never re-establish her relationship with her daughter-in-law, her son and even their kids.

Bernie, left fatherless at an early age, had become my closest cousin friend, going to the Afro-centered jazz clubs I liked so much and often double-dating with me in my last year of high school and New Jersey-New York life. Perhaps the breakup and reunion with Maxine explained why he became so conservative and closed in his last years, a man whose Zionist and anti-minority attitudes led him to become more and more reactionary and unscrupulous as the years went by. The fact that his son was a pro-basketball trainer, who made his living by attending to the physical woes of his mainly Black players, didn't prevent the father from spreading venom about African Americans as well as Latinos on Facebook and emails. A true Jewish Neo-con he broadcast a known lie about Palestinian anti-semitism on Facebook. And when I called him on the lie, he wrote me that maybe I was right, but he found it a useful tidbit to sway his anti-Arab followers, and therefore he wouldn't detract his message. At that point, I withdrew from his Facebook group, and never tried to see him again.

As for his mother, my aunt Ellie was embittered and branded by the alienation she suffered from son and family for the rest of her life. Once when I visited her lonely apartment in Fort Lauderdale, she showed me the pictures of Bernie and his family. "I hardly ever see them," she told me, "but these are my memories. They're always with me as I prepare for my end."

5. Ernie

I got to know several Black students on the freshman football team. The Blacks and Italians combined votes with the Jewish to win me the presidency of the school in my senior year. I knew one kind of swishy Black student who was singled out for jokes, mockery and abuse; I knew another student Roger who stood out for quality and caliber and who his fellow Blacks called Sidney Portier. There was another Black student who sang calyso and they called him Hairy Bananafante. Most of the Black kids were into R&B and do-wap, which lots of white kids, Jews and Italians included, tried to imitate.

Nat King Cole, Billy Eckstein, Sammy Davis Jr., Sarah Vaughn and yes, Lady Day, were among my favorite singers—all these Black dieties of my New York/New Jersey youth (though yes Sinatra remained number 1, and I had a special thing for Mel Torme's jazz singing when he sang Fred Astaire songs, or even when he sang songs from *Porgy and Bess*).

But the figure who stands out among all the African Americans I knew and who helped shape my life in my early years was my father's employee, Ernie Wilson. Perhaps my relationship with Ernie was the most important of all my experiences of Blackness in my high school years. For here was one of the people I was most close to in my adolescence in New Jersey, the Black man who became my teacher and, I felt, older friend, working as we did on catering job after catering job, the one who, when my flat feet and ankles could stand the dishwashing and schlepping no more, would sometimes have to help me walk to the truck and drive me back home before calling it a night.

Tall and slim, with a trim moustache and athletic body, Ernie had come to work in the catering kitchen of our family's restaurant even while he was a sophomore in a nearby college. Now the restaurant was going to take considerable time and energy, and the brothers decided to leave my mother's brother, Benny, in charge of the catering's day-to-day operations while Ernie would be his right-hand man. Over the years, even before entering high school, I became that right hand man's right hand man so that the trio became the core of the catering business going to synagogues, homes and other venues to handle the setup, the basic kitchen work and breakdown for parties small or grand.

I guess you could call it a great arrangement. I earned the money for a car, gas and charges for dates and lone incursions to the theaters and jazz clubs of New York, even as I put some money aside for college. That I was the boss's son did little to affect how I was treated on the job, as my father and uncle made it quite clear that I was Uncle Benny's second assistant, which really meant that I was completely beholden to Ernie, the most important Black person employed in the overall food business. I sometimes resented my constant stream of work assignments while the better-off Jewish boys around me hardly ever worked, but simply lived off liberal allowances from doting parents, going to parties and making out with girls I perhaps would have liked to be with. However, I did enjoy the freedom my money brought me and actually loved working with Ernie, especially when the party was over, the van was packed and we were ready to go.

I loved working with him, because coming or going, once he was in the van, he became king. He knew how to drive it beautifully, smoothly and still fast, even with precarious loads of tables, bottles, dishes and glasses, as well as all the food and drinks needed to make a party work. He always played R&B on the radio, so I got to know about all the singers and groups even when my own tastes turned to jazz; he always left early enough to expore alternative routes so we got to know every nook and cranny of the garden state.

Meantime Ernie talked to me about all the trials and tribulations of being Black in America and New Jersey—all the troubles he had, he and his wife had, and they and their kids had getting through week by week on a salary that just didn't meet their needs.

"Don't get me wrong," he'd say, "I'm not complaining about your dad. He and Al are good bosses, they pay me way above the market price, they give me plenty of overtime and bonuses too. I figure with all I've learned from them and Benny, I could pretty much run a catering business of my own if I could put together the capital. But no one's going to get that kind of money with my kinda job, which gives me enough to live on if I'm careful, though not enough to get ahead. I'm happy I got work, 'cause Lord knows there's lots a' brothers in my neighborhood who don't have a damned thing. But I pay my rent and I get to use the truck even when we don't have a job. I mean I'm happy I got Jewish bosses who respect their help and give us a living wage, but I'm kinda caught in a rut and I got to figure how to get out."

Just listening to Ernie made me feel I could begin to understand the lives of poor people, especially Black ones. Sometimes we would swing by Ernie's house on the way to or from a catering gig, so I got to see Elizabeth Port, where most of the city's Black population lived. I got to see the rundown houses, the unemployed men standing on corners, the beat up bars, the barbershops, the soul food barbecue stands. I sometimes entered Ernie's rundown home, met his wife and soon their first child, as she took her early steps on the boards of their living room floor, covered with tired threadbare rugs and beatup furniture. I used the bathroom more than once and saw my reflection stare out of the battered mirror revealing the plaster cracked wall behind me—Mel, in poverty: an image which was to stay with me all my life and fill me with fear during the long periods when, even after my doctoral degree, I would be out of work, alone and poor.

One day, Ernie and I traveled down to south Jersey to deliver some catered goods. And with virtually the whole day ahead of us, we travelled from town to town, almost the whole length of the small state back up to Elizabeth. I was familiar with Black poverty areas in my home area, but now Ernie made a point of cruising every downtown and ghetto area from Red Hook and Long Branch up through Trenton and New Brunswick. Ernie showed me all the Black neighborhoods, which seemed so terribly poor and segregated. I felt like we were touring the rural south.

"Yeah," said Ernie, "It sure tells you who we are and how little we've come from the deep south to the south of Newark. And how many of us died in World War II and Korea? And where are we going from here?"

Of course, much of my adult life, in spite of all its middle class trappings, would be spent among the poor, working for and with the poor, teaching the poor and sometimes writing about the poor as well. And at least some of my early writing and my work in the theater would be related to the Black poor, and then the Latin American and Latino poor, so that so much of my work and writing had their beginnings in my short-lived but important relationship with Ernie.

In the few years I knew Ernie, I watched the man who became almost an older brother, who taught me so much at work, who, at my father's urging spent some working hours helping my Uncle Benny teach an inept boy how to drive. But Ernie did more, telling me about condoms and even how to buy them without being too embarrassed, telling me about girls and how Black guys dealt with them—telling me why Black people were proud of their jazz musicians in spite of their drugs and then cluing him in to the fact that most Black people claimed to like their uppity jazz music more than they really did. But the biggest and worst thing Ernie taught me was about the terrible downward slide of a life.

He had been a football star in high school and even got some months in college until he got hurt. No longer useful in football, he soon found out his limitations as a student and had to drop out. After that he drifted from little job to little job until he got the catering job and began his upward swing, getting married, having his first child and renting his first apartment, however sparse and humble.

But somehow as I got ready to go to college, Ernie peaked and declined. I only saw bits in the overall process, but I did encounter a few moments when I could sense the downward arc reflected on Ernie's face and I could all but feel some of the bitterness that marked a trajectory that went down the hill of hope as life turned into the bleak and cruel thing it is for most who walk the earth. Perhaps the very key turning point in his decline and his life was at a moment of seeming victory when I returned from my last high school spring break college-scouting trip and I stopped by to see Ernie and Uncle Benny not in the catering kitchen, but in the parking lot where they were looking over a shiny new light blue Chevy that turned out to be the first new car Ernie had ever owned.

"Hey, this Chevy's great, Ernie. Take me for a ride," I begged, and sure enough Ernie drove me around. At first, he glowed showing off the car's power by revving up the motor and passing a couple of cars.

"This is great," I repeated.

"Well but it don't have a lot of extras," he said. "Your dad helped get me a good deal but I just didn't have enough to get air conditioning or better seats or even a radio."

"But you can get them, Ernie, maybe over time."

"Yeah, over time," he repeated and then returned quickly to the parking lot, letting me off.

"You better get ready for college, you don't wanna drop out like me and end up without an a/c with the summer comin' on," Ernie told me, cutting the conversation short and getting out of his car.

Those last weeks of high school were a wild, irregular time involving a trip on the Hudson and all kinds of parties. One of them took some of the Jewish and other white kids down to Elizabeth Port and the house of one of the Black students. There, we danced to R&B in a scene that could have could have been out of *Hairspray*, with lots of competition on the dance floor and a few flirtations that crossed the color line. For me, it was a major moment of my coming of age. But when I told Ernie about it the day after the party, the reaction was far from the positive one I'd expected.

"Now what you doing going down to our side of town? Don't you know how dangerous we be? And this line-crossing bullshit, that's just as phoney and foolish as phoney and foolish can be. You'll forget all this when you leave us behind and get of town, Mr. College Boy."

Of course, we continued to work together on catering jobs as I was trying to build up my college war chest, and as I got my rejections and offers and made my decisions about where to go. On some of their catering runs, I began to sense a new negative tone to our interactions. Ernie was shorter with me, less talkative, more grim. One Friday, I took off with my father to New Haven for my last college interview—at Yale, where, overwhelmed by the buildings and the tone of things, I sensed I was really in over his head.

On our return, my father and I somehow got to talking about the catering business and then about Ernie, with me telling my father how great Ernie had been to me all this time., but how I now sensed something big troubling him.

And then my father turned to me and said, "I don't know. Ever since he got that car, he's been offkey, coming in late, squabbling with Benny, and the worst of it: he's often got liquor on his breath. I just don't know where this is heading."

I asked, "Have you talked to him?"

"Not much, although I did tell him I wasn't happy about his coming in late, just when we were considering a big raise for him."

"Maybe the raise would help get him back on track."

"But how can I reward him when he's screwing up?"

I tried to defend my suggestion, but my father went further.

"Look, I understand we all need a sense of future and maybe buying that car just told him that even though this should've been a positive thing, it just pointed out how limited his future was. We got him the sweetest deal and even gave him a special bonus that helped cover the down payment and more. The raise I was going to give him was to help him with the payments and get the extras he wanted for the car. But I'm telling you, all that's on the line now."

Sure enough, on the next catering job, Ernie showed up late and in bad humor, clearly drunk and bitter.

"Look at my car," he told me as he pulled out of the lot. "My first new car and it's a piece of shit, and everyone knows it too—the poorest brothers on the block are laughing about it," he said. "Everything about it's cheap, it just shows me how I've gone nowhere working here."

"But I heard my dad helped you out," I argued.

"I don't want no help," Ernie said. "I'm thirty-four years old. And I don't want no help from him or any white man, Jewish or whatever. I want to make it on my own. But I ain't never gonna make it—I can see that now. You goin' off to college and little Ernie still in the kitchen with your Uncle Benny, and neither of us able to get anywhere here in this place." That night he had a bit of a run-in with Benny on the job, and he rode home bitterly, turning up the R&B, and unwilling to talk, as he stared straight ahead and occasionally opened the window to send some spit down the road.

Off I went to college and when I came back for Christmas break, I went over to the catering kitchen only to see that Ernie and his car weren't there. "What's happened to Ernie?" I asked Uncle Benny.

"You don't want to know, Mel. A couple of weeks ago, someone vandalized Ernie's car, twisting off the mirrors, gouging the metal, flatting the tires. Not a week later the car was repossessed. Seems he was spending his money on liquor and women, and some of his neighbors thought he was getting uppity so they did what they could to bring him down. He stopped showing up to work when he should, and when he did show he was drunk and nasty. I asked your dad to call a meeting with him to see what we could do, but he showed up late and drunker than ever, and started shouting at us that he was sick of it all and was quitting."

Uncle Benny was almost in tears as he told all this. "I love Ernie," he told me, "I've always wanted the best for him, and then he was like a stick that someone or something starts to bend until it breaks in two. It killed me to see him go, but I know he had to." It was at that point that I hugged my sweet uncle tightly to me. We both cried, thinking of Ernie and knowing there was little or nothing we could do.

And strange or logically enough, it occurred to me that the same thing that had happened to Ernie might well be happening to my uncle, if only because of all my father had bled from the restaurant. But this is Ernie's story, so I don't want to get into that. I do remember going with my uncle over to Ernie's house, but there was no sign of him, his family or his car. "They couldn't pay their rent, so they moved out one night," a neighbor told us. "And no one seems to know where to."

Mel's Cultural Turns and All That Jazz

Perhaps it all began with his school taking him to the opera or, more probably, his parents taking him to all those New York musicals—they were only off on Wednesdays so they'd pick him up at junior and then senior high school and off he'd go to see one musical or another: *Brigadoon, Finnegan's Rainbow, Kiss Me Kate, South Pacific, Damn Yankees, Wish You Were Here, Miss Liberty* or whatever. Later he started going to the theater on his own, or sometimes taking a date, to see plays on and off-Broadway: O'Neill's *Long Day's Journey* and the revival of *The Iceman Cometh*; to see Miller's *Crucible* and *View from the Bridge,* Williams' Tallulah-damned revival of *Streetcar, his Cat on a Hot Tin Roof,* or *Suddenly Last Summer*—to even see Lotte Lenya in the revival of *Three Penny Opera,* to see Albee's *Zoo Story,* Leroy Jones' *Dutchman,* or even Beckett's *Waiting for Godot. (West Side Story* opened some days after he went off to college).

And of course he'd started to read—the plays of course, but also *Portrait of the Artist, Sons and Lovers,* but also *Women in Love* (did he understand any of it?). Lawrence was his king of sex, love and the passionate life, made even more so by his fictive presence in Aldous Huxley's *Point Counter Point.* And then he read Rimbaud, Dostoyevsky, Kafka, a hundred other things by so many writers from so many places…

Then there were those ethnic radio day programs—like "The Life of Riley," "Amos n Andy" or "Luigi" or "Mollie Goldberg"; and then came tv with Uncle Milt and Walter Cronkite, with Jimmy Durante, Jackie Gleason, Lucille Ball and even Desi Arnaz, with Ernie Kovacs and Edie Adams, and then the wonderful Imogene Coca and the greatest of the great, Sid Cesar. And of course, Sid was king, his comic routines like jazz solos roaring and crackling through the New Jersey nights.

Still, in the loneliest times of his post-Ellen years, it was the radio DJ shows, and no longer the top twenty ones, but those less commercial but top quality figures who enriched his life. First there was William B. Williams, who once pointed out how Fred Astaire could look good in a purple shirt, a yellow tie, and green jacket, and who taught him what jazz was, by insisting that, maybe short of Louie, Ella and Lady Day, the post-Ava, Nelson-Riddled Sinatra was the greatest living jazz singer even though he rarely if ever set out to sing jazz. He remembers as Williams played Sinatra's "I've Got You Under your Skin," with an incredible trombone solo, and then the whole *Wee Small Hours* album cracked his love-starved world.

Gradually Mel left pop behind (no Elvis, no doo-wop, no Rock Around the Clock, no Earth Angel—and no dancing either) as modern post-Parker hardbop jazz became the center of his teenage life. Starting with William B., it spread and deepened with Symphony Sid and his return to the New York airwaves. Sid had an hour right after William B, and Mel would choose that hour to leave the house and drive alone south toward Rahway and beyond, almost always turning around at the half hour mark, to make it home at program's end. With Sid, it was old timers like Duke Ellington, Count Basie, Coleman Hawkins, Lester Young, Roy Eldridge. But then it was Diz and the Bird, Sonny Stitt, Sonny Rollins and the young John Coltrane; it was Errol Garner, Horace Silver, Max Roach and Clifford Brown; it was Milt Jackson and the Modern Jazz Quartet.

On the radio at night, finally, he listened to Jean Sheppard improvising his great nostalgic stories of U.S.A. life, taking us out of the fifties and propelling us toward the sixties and beyond. Each night Jean weaved his magic, as if he were another jazz musician, but his medium was words, and those words rang loud and clear as he told us about the difference between the day people who seemed to rule the world, and the visionary night people, the right people to understand the new world that was being born out of the rejection of the old.

Then one night, Jean went all the way—long before Howard Beale in *Network*—as he called out along the airways for all his fellow night people 'to put their radios on open windowsills and turn up the volume, loud enough for the neighbors next door to hear: 'I'm as mad as hell and I'm not going to take this anymore!'" Night after night he called out for the night people to rise and more and more Mel wished to join them, to leave his high school world and all the Jewish girls behind him—to fully enter the world of jazz to express his anger about the world around him, about his decision not to take it any more and to find his way toward a new life in the night world of jazz—a world keyed by Jean's byword which he called out in every broadcast, "*Excelsior*!" he urged his listeners on, as Mel and all the night people found their way.

Mel remembers going over to Mike Marcus' house to listen to Benny Goodman's "Sing Sing Sing," with Gene Krupa, Harry James and the others. He remembers Mike taking out the American song book and playing Ellington, Carmichael, Porter and then all the Jewish songwriters, as Mel tried to sing all the songs he could, until Mike, maybe tiring from Mel's strained efforts, told him, "Mel, if you really want to learn about jazz, you should visit Marty Adams, because he's really into it."

So Mel sought out the big gawky Anglo kid who he'd never talked to before because his dad was the head of the Board of Education and that automatically made Marty off-limits. Wasn't he a day person if there ever was one? How strange to enter the patrician family parlor, to hear Charlie Parker's recordings and see Marty get out his sax and play along the Bird's solo lines, and then to hear Sonny Stitt and other Bird followers.

"You've gotta get an instrument and learn to play this stuff to really appreciate what they're doing," he told Mel. "And maybe you need to drink some booze and smoke some reefer too." And then he said some things that to Mel were far more remarkable

"The whole thing is creativity, invention. Forget the melody just play on the chord patterns—and watch, soon they won't play white Tin Pan Alley, they'll create and play on their own songs, like Ellington, and then they'll drop the chord pattern and just take off. That's where Bird was going. He didn't get there but that's where we're going. Soon, the tyranny of the 78s and 45s will die and the musicians can play on and on until they go spiraling off the face of the earth. And Black musicians will lead the way, because they've suffered to create it, they've been at it and explored each and every corner of it, but there'll be great musicians of every color and ethnicity. Clearly the ethnic whites'll be cool, the Jews, the Italians, but the others too, even white boys like me and Japanese guys and maybe some guys from the moon. Right now there's a whole Latin thing happening in New York, and hardly any jazz fans know it's happening."

Mel fought back, he argued that maybe the freedom would be too extreme. Ensemble work would suffer, the freedom would turn to chaos without limits, and no one would be able to follow the music, all the musicians would get Ph.D.'s and the music's roots would whither away not with a bang but we both knew what. "Rollins and Miles create a masterpiece in a few measures. What would happen if they could play on and on? Jazz is blues applied," he argued, "and if you go too far from blues, the jazz will die."

So the arguments went, but more important than all this speculation was Mel's parents getting him a beat up Chevy, and his now constant trips from Elizabeth alone and with others to the wide range of bars and clubs spread across Manhattan. Mel began with Birdland in Midtown where the bebop revolution still found a home first with Bird himself, and then Miles, Lee Konitz, Gerry Muligan and others virtually gave birth to the cool, though more and more the club bored Mel with George Shearing and Toots Thielemans, but intrigued him with the ever-more elegant Modern Jazz Quartet, as vibes player Milt Jackson bluesed his way through one-handed John Lewis' stylish inventions. Once in awhile Dizzy and other Parkerites still played the club, rattling the walls with post bebop, and one night Mel waved to Diz as he went passing by, congratulating the great trumpeter on his band's sound and introducing his oh-too-pretty date. Dizzy surprised them by sitting down at their table and offering to order them drinks. Mel was pleased and his date impressed, but he sensed that the Diz might be trying to birddog his date, and turned down the drinks, getting up and saying they had to get going.

"Maybe he'd've invited us to one of those late night sessions up in Harlem," she chided.

"You, maybe, but me, I'm not so sure" Mel muttered and decided to jazz it on his own in the future.

Mel tried the Metropole and Basin Street, but they were too traditional and clearly not the cutting-edge places he sought. Finally he discovered the Village and thereabouts, exploring the key clubs in the area.

Café Bohemia, at 15 Barrow Street, was a 100-seat "progressive jazz" club that had been built for Parker; but when the Bird died it was where Art Blakey's Jazz Messengers performed, followed by Miles and a young tenor sax player named Coltrane, still completely unknown, along with Red Garland, Paul Chambers, and Philly Joe Jones in a group now known as the first Great Quintet, playing together in July of 1955, with Miles sounding as lyrical as the young Mozart, and Coltrane sounding as wild as an unhinged Beethoven—like maybe Berlioz.

One night Max Roach and Art Blakey as well as their sidemen showed up, and so did Rollins, Cannonball Adderley, and the kings, Monk and Mingus —they all came by and crammed the Bohemia stage for a jam session that filled the air with the brightest sounds of the fifties. And Mel knew it, he was living the dream of the night people—the dream of great creativity and freedom, the great constellation of music occurring at the same time as the rush of abstract expressionism, happenings and pop art, and, yes, Latin and Caribbean music was peaking and New York displaced Paris as the Capital of the world.

Mel kept on working for his dad's catering service and restaurant, always earning enough for the gas and a few drinks, as he kept on exploring the local jazz scene. After Miles left Bohemia, he went time and again to the Village Vanguard, at first to hear some of the top vocalists like June Christy, Chris Connor, and Carmen McRae—but also comics like Mort Sahl and Lenny Bruce, and then even writers like Jack Keruoac and Alan Ginsburg reading as musicians tried to figure out what to play.

Above all, there were the Vanguard's jam sessions on Sunday afternoons out of the glare of the summer sun, where Lee Konitz, Warne Marsh, Zoot Sims and Stan Getz. Then came Art Blakey's Messengers of 1956-57 featuring Donald Bird on trumpet, Jackie McLean on alto sax, and Ira Sullivan on tenor. And through it all, the 6th Avenue subway constantly passed and rattled the walls drowning out all the performers every few minutes. (Fifty years later, it was the same subway and the same rattling walls, but all the old performers were gone).

But the most crucial adventures were those he experienced at the Half Note west of the Village on Hudson and the Five Spot east of the Village on the edge of the Bowery near Cooper Union. Charlie Mingus held court at the Half Note, with Danny Richmond on drums and Charlie Rouse on sax. Manic and explosive, Mingus was at his creative peak blasting away on bass and even piano, bringing in new music and new musicians almost nightly, working with the musicians as they came to understand what he had in mind even as they performed before a live audience. So many stylistic dimensions emerged, from gospel to soul to funk, all with an Ellington flair. "Fables of Faubus" seemed a perfect satiric answer to segregation, his "Better Get it in Your Soul" like a revival turned orgiastic. Two classically trained cellists joined him to play out some baroque-styled blues. A trained flamenco dancer jumped on a table and danced away to Mingus' brilliant flamenco-blues synthesis. Performance was king at the Half Note. Mingus never sounded as brilliant on records as he did in the club. Mel returned night after night.

And the only musician to stand with and maybe above Miles and Mingus was Thelonious Monk, who came out of prison and began playing at the Five Spot.. There were always drunks outside asking for handouts and it cost a dollar to get in, to see the greatest jazz pianist and composer of the moment. Playing his piano stride and Ellington-style, pausing, breaking patterns, creating dissonances, cutting across his sax men—Rollins, Coltrane, Charlie Rouse (later it would be Yusef Latif and Johnny Griffith), Monk laid down his chords, played his solo, cut to the side out the door for dope or who knew what, then bounced back in and played another set of chords, mixing or breaking spurts of inspiration, remaking his own compositions, or making others' compositions his own. And almost all of those present knew they were hearing some jazz equivalent of Schoenberg and Bartok—a form of chamber jazz more rooted and more brilliant than anything any other players were able to generate. And Mel knew he was hearing the apotheosis of all he ever wanted out of music and life.

In perhaps two short years, Mel visited these and other clubs and saw these and many other musicians. Then too he went to concerts at Town and Carnegie Halls, as well as at festivals as often as and whenever possible. He saw Louis, saw Ella, saw Lady Day in her last days. He saw trombonist J.J. Johnson, classy pianists

Dave Brubeck and Don Shirley, flautist Bud Shank and flugelhorn player Don Ellis on and on and on and on. He began with the raucous Jazz at the Philharmonic concerts at the Essex House in his birth town of Newark. But perhaps the most notable festival and the last one he attended was on Rikers Island in the summer of 1957, just weeks after his high school graduation and before he went off to college, where the musicians seemed to be saying goodbye to him as hard bop slid into soul and funk and yes, jazz began the path that Marty Adams had signaled to him some time during 1955. But then it was off to college and the end of his core jazz world.

"If I could write one story, one piece," he told himself "that could reach where Mingus and Monk are going, one which opens up to all that is dischordant and offtime, and brings it home in a new time and new space where everything, in spite of everything, comes together at last, then that would make it worthwhile to have lived."

Of course he knew that for many of them drugs were a key part of it all. And some of his favorite musicians succumbed as Parker and others had succumbed before them. Was it true that the drugs let them reach new heights, or was that a myth invented to justify the drugs? It was somehow part of the brilliant corners, turns and riffs that made the music of that time so great.

Whatever the truth of the matter was, he knew that he had somehow lucked in on a creative whirlwind that could rarely find an equivalent. And this jazz became a model for all he would ever hope to do in writing. And it probably was the mark of what he would fail to do.

In the many years which followed, he often said, "Those crazy two years ruined me for jazz. I would never be seventeen again, and jazz would never be as good as that again. Some great nights over the years, but really all a comedown. I was blessed and cursed as I came of age and graduated in those years so soon after the death of the Bird."

A New Jersey Boy and His Year at Dartmouth

So graduation came, the parties and the long hot summer. He didn't try Princeton, where Ellen's boyfriend was going. But he was accepted by Brown and Dartmouth and decided to go for the old Indian school after he'd visited the campus green, so attractive with the snowmelt and heard from a well-known *New York Times* book reviewer, Carlos Baker, that Dartmouth was better for a would be writer. Could that be?

Soon he arrived and they placed a freshman beanie on his head, told him about Dartmouth ways, took him around campus and town as he began to realize what it meant to be virtually without women in the middle of what was for him nowhere. Within a day, he met his two dorm roommates and realized he had virtually nothing in common with them, one an Anglo prep school kid, the other a redheaded Irish kid from the south. Both planned studying sciences and were as dry as reeds without water.

Sputnick was the rage. Sherman Adams came to campus and spoke about the glories of science and their contribution. Everything seemed WASP Republican. Even the campus poet, Richard Eberhardt, fit the mold. Robert Frost, the ideal poet for this crowd, made his appearance, but hovered over the campus literary life, the king of all the lesser super-Anglo writers, with John Ciardi the respectable Italian-American exception especially with his translation of Dante.

An old man who'd never published a thing but was an alumnus from the Depression needing a job and was therefore hired to teach the English course he was required to take—*The Dartmouth Bible* and Shakespeare, as the students wrote one miserable paper after another. The Sociology class was immense with some 300 students, a lecturer and god knew how many TAs, with the professor insisting they read Marquand's *Point of Now Return* so they'd learn how low Dartmouth was on the insurance company

CEO totem pole. The French class was terrible, with Villon, yes, but Ronsard, Boileau and other assorted drags. The Philosophy class dealt with the straight British tradition from Bacon to Russell as if Sartre, Camus and others he admired meant nothing at all. The Astronomy class was farcical with an old Russian teacher who spoke an indecipherable, Khrushchev-sounding English, as he scribbled diagrams on the backboard with splatches of chalk dust all but covering the same thoroughly whitened black suit he insisted on wearing day after day.

There seemed little redemption in it all, as the white boys went off to play tennis until the weather gave, and then switched to skis as the fall turned toward winter so that, once shoveled, the sidewalks became tunnels of snow piled high above one's head. Mel looked around and saw white/white/white with only a few Jewish kids who all seemed from wealthy East Coast families, and only one southern-accented Jewish son of a Charleston rabbi being someone he half-related to until that relatable someone apparently felt far more alienated and lost than Mel and committed suicide just after Christmas break.

As for Black and Latino kids, there were very few, and he hardly got to meet them in his first months at the college. And as for women, the situation was simply deplorable. Every time a woman came into the cafeteria, all the boys tapped on the side of their glasses. Every time there was a special weekend the boys invited up girlfriends and then fought to keep sober enough to prevent their dates being swept away according to the revered custom of "bird-dogging" so common to the college. Meantime, some of the rich guys went after "town girls," nurses, shop girls and whatnot, hoping for sex and then a marriage to an eligible waspy girl from another elite private college.

He for his part found a friend in a young man who played jazz piano in the dining room adjacent to the cafeteria. At times, he listened; at times he sang along as the sessions grew longer and more intense. His other great refuge was the Baker library where he studied Weber and Marx while eyeing and finally getting caught up in the fine Orozco murals which portrayed the world from the flood, through the Mexican Revolution and on into the New England present—with a striking Christ having cut down his cross staring diamond-eyed at him as he stared back from his reading table.

He also retreated to the town's one movie theater, where he watched one film after another, and finally signed on as the theater's paid critic, with the rub being that he had to review and rate the movies before they arrived in Hanover for him to see, so that the standard dishonest procedure was to find the *New York Times* review and use it as a source for the paragraph he was supposed to write and the rating he was supposed to provide. The day came soon enough when he couldn't find a review for "Underwater Warrior" and made up one indicating that the film dealt with Caesar, Napoleon and Hitler acting out their military victories in a series of water ballets, each hoping to prove he was best, with the winner murdering his rivals. (He gave the film a .0001 rating, used the letters IBM as his identifying signature, and was immediately relieved of his position.

Meanwhile, he had to write his Bible paper and wrote "an unstageable play," "All the World in Bibleland," which lay bare biblical contradictions and presented D.H. Lawrence and Einstein as featured players in a star-filled cast of thousands. He also wrote a paper showing the indebtedness of Ibsen's *Master Build*er to *Macbeth*. How impressed was his teacher, who wrote a formal letter commending the play and submitted it to the student literary journal, *The Dartmouth Quarterly*?

He went home for Christmas and then for Spring break, enjoying seeing friends and going to the Village for New York jazz once again, only to learn that his parents were selling their interest in the restaurant and moving to California to make a new life near their daughter and grandchildren.

"Why don't you come out for the summer?" his father asked. "You've friends there and it would be a good change of pace."

He realized that he'd have no place to stay in Elizabeth, so it seemed the best thing to do. His father got him permission to bring the Mercury to Hanover with the promise he wouldn't use it until it was time to go. So he drove it up to Dartmouth and parked his car in an assigned parking lot where it was to stay until he was ready for the westward trip.

No sooner had he returned to campus when he got word that his play had won the Freshman Writing Award, and he was invited to the next meeting of *The Dartmouth Quarterly*. Off he went, and found himself congratulated and invited to be on the editorial board. Only a few other people were there. Above all he remembers the brilliant editor David Viscott, a Jewish kid from Scarsdale who would become famous as a pop radio psychologist who promoted risk taking as a way of life until his early death from a heart attack. He also remembers Alden Van Buskirk, a strange young man from Saint Louis who wore unmatching socks and would have a day in the sun as a poet only to die a few years later. At first, they spoke of the *villanelle* and other poetic forms, but they then did a critique of the materials for the upcoming issue and asked him if had anything. He said he would go over a story of his "Shadows," to see if they wanted it.

It was only then that things got fully serious as Viscott pointed to the low literary quality of this Sputnick generation, and also the depolitization of poetry as part of the nation's rampant anti-communism. "Now we have a special problem. Because we want to encourage political writing, but we don't want to encourage dogmatic garbage and bigotry. And it turns out that Dartmouth's student program committee has just approved a huge sum for a big semester-ending poetry read and Q&A featuring David Wang."

Mel asked who Wang was. And Viscott told him, "He's a Chinese American poet, a class of '55 alumnus, who's fallen for Ezra Pound's craziest ideas, favoring racial segregation and euthanasia."

"Now he's formed his own organization, 'North American Citizens for the Constitution' and he's been going all around the Ivy League promoting his rot." said Buskirk.

"And they're using student monies provided by you, me and the few minority students on campus to bring him in," Viscott added.

"But this is rotten," Mel said.

"Yes, but it's a position some of these white Republican lunkheads here might just like."

"So, what should we do?"

"We should attack him, or at least join with the coalition that will try to mess up his agenda."

"That's fine with me," Mel said. And he joined with his new friends in their overall opposition to Wang's presentation. It was the evening of the day that Mel's Bibleland play appeared in the journal, when Wang, his burly bodyguards and a few of his groupies arrived in two white Cadillac limousines in front of the stately Dartmouth Hall, where the poet was scheduled to speak. A crowd was already there at the front double doors leading to campus auditorium, gathered, with Wang's supporters and detractors entering into a shouting match that threatened to turn violent when a squadron of motorcycle cops roared into the parking area and cleared a space for the poet and his group to enter, as the auditorium filled to capacity.

A Dartmouth representative welcomed the audience, spoke of the college's great tradition of free speech, and warned the crowd that the police were under instructions to arrest anyone disrupting or signaling potential violence. Cheers and boos followed, but then the lights went down and some bombastic music came up that stopped everyone in their tracks as the poet stepped forward read some of his race-baiting Pound-like cantos while spewing venom at kikes, queers and commies.

At this point, Mel joined his new *Quarterly* friends as they raced to the platform, seized a microphone, and began reading virulent passages directly from Pound's Cantos. When Wang supporters tried to shout them down, the literati began reading from the new *Quarterly* issue, with Mel reading the most anti-racist passages from his play, with the poet's supporters cursing and braying and the cops finally rushed to the platform to cut off the loudspeakers, push the literati to one side, and whisk Wang and his entourage out of the auditorium into their awaiting vehicles.

Mel thrilled to his own participation as he and his new friends saw Wang and his Wangites drive off in their Cadillac limousines, without the poet's ever having laid out his full racist case. The Cadillacs disappeared into the night, with Mel feeling that this was surely the most meaningful moment of his entire freshman year at Dartmouth.

Soon after, Mel took his exams writing papers on European history, on Dreiser, Fitzgerald, Hemingway, Faulkner, and other writers—but not Below, Malamud or Roth; then he began preparations for his trip to California, thinking he would return but never going back except for the rarest visit in the more than sixty years he was to live after he left the East Coast.

If the family of Faulkner's Quentin Compson had enough to stake him to one year at Harvard before he committed suicide, so Mel and his family had enough on hand to finance him for one year at Dartmouth before he committed what amounted to ethnic suicide (or was it affirmation?) first moving out west, and then north, but finally turning south.

ABOUT MARC ZIMMERMAN

Marc Zimmerman is Professor Emeritus of Latin American and Latino Studies at the University of Illinois in Chicago (UIC) as well as World Cultures and Literatures and Hispanic Studies at the University of Houston, where he served as chair (2002-2008), involving considerable work with Latin American Studies programs. Zimmerman served in Nicaragua's Ministerio de Cultura during the first year of the Sandinista Revolution. He has been director of Global CASA/ LACASA Books since 1998; and he has written and edited over forty books on world, Latin American and Latino cultural and literary studies. He has won Fulbright, Rockefeller, Puerto Rican Studies and other major awards; he has served on the jury of Cuba's Casa de la Américas, and been guest professor at McGill U., as wells as universities in Madrid, Puerto Rico, Nicaragua, and Tucumán, Argentina.

While Zimmerman holds a Ph.D. in Comparative Literature from the U. of California San Diego, he also holds an M.A. in Creative Writing from San Francisco State U., where he studied with Walter Van Tilburg Clark, Herbert Blau, Irving Halperin, Mark Harris, James Scheville, Ray West, and Herbert Wilner. His early stories were published in *The Dartmouth Quarterly*, *Descant*, *The Great River Review,* and (in translation) *Nuova Prosa*, a key fiction journal in Milan, Italy. More recent stories have appeared in the Chicago Latino online journal, *El BeiSMan*, as well as in *Voices in Italian Americana* and *Literal*, a Latin American literary journal.

In 2023, Zimmerman published his book on the rise of Chicago Mexican and Chicano writing; and he continues coordinating the development of a series of interviews and related materials entitled "The Chicago Latino Artist Series Project (CLASP)," which he donated to the Smithsonian American Art History Collection. Based on this ongoing work, Zimmerman has thus far published books and CDs centered on Chicago Mexican artists José Gamaliel González (2010 and 2013), Aaron Kerlow (2015) and José Guerrero (2016); he has presented and published work on Chicago Central American and Puerto Rican art, as he develops a book based on his Chicago Latino art research.

Returning to his first love of creative writing, Zimmerman has also been developing a book series of books of "autofiction" (related life-based stories, dreams and fantasies organized into novel-like structures), *Illusions of Memory* touching on Jewish, Italian, African and Central American, but above all Mexican/Chicano, Central American and Puerto Rican themes—with eleven books published and several others in progress, and with four volumes translated into Spanish and one into Italian.

In recent years, Zimmerman has lectured on Chicago Latino art at Dartmouth College, the U. of California Berkeley and San Diego, Purdue U., and the Universidad de Costa Rica. He has read from his fiction in Italy at Milano's Verso Bookstore and the Torino International Book Fair, in California at the University Press Book Store in Berkeley, the Tía Chucha Cultural Center and Pop-Hop Books in the L.A. area, the Media Center in San Diego, the Avid Reader in Davis, and the Green Arcade in San Francisco—as well as in public libraries in East Los Angeles and La Jolla. In Chicago, he has read for the Palabra Pura program of the Guild Complex, the Heirloom Bookstore, the Lozano Public Library, 18th Street Casa Cultural and Pilsen Community Books. In Puerto Rico, he has read at Librería Laberinto in San Juan and Librería Candil in Ponce, as well as in a seminar at El Centro de Estudios Avanzados in El Viejo San Juan. For additional presentations, he may be reached at tel. (281) 513-9475 or mzimmerman1939@gmail.com. To visit his author's website and above all his Illusions of Memory series, visit www.marczimmerman.net.

He and his wife Esther Soler from Quebradillas, Puerto Rico, divide each year between the island and the Wicker Park/ Humboldt Park area of Chicago. They continue to travel each year to Minnesota and California—to Mexico, Europe, and wherever else they can.

Cycle III: 1981 - ?? (forthcoming)

The In-Between Years (1980-1988)

The Solid Years. Chicago, Puerto Rico, Guatemala World *(1988-2001)*

Houston, Puerto Rico and the World (2001-2011)

The Not So Golden Years. Chicago, Puerto Rico and the Writer's Life *(2011-?)*